Bewohnte Natur

Living with Nature

Edition DETAIL

Hinaus aufs Land! Warum es Städter in die Natur zieht

Let's go to the countryside! Why city dwellers are drawn to nature

Sandra Hofmeister

Noch nie war die Sehnsucht nach Natur größer als heute – in einer Zeit, in der immer mehr Menschen in Städten wohnen. Das Land gilt als unberührter Erholungsraum und die Natur als ein Ort des Ursprünglichen, an dem sich das Ich vom Stress in der Großstadt ausruhen und zu sich selbst finden kann. Auf dem Land zu wohnen, auch wenn nur am Wochenende oder in den Ferien, ist für viele Städter ein Traum. Je mehr sie in ihren Großstadtalltag eingebunden sind, desto größer wird ihr Verlangen nach einer Alternative. So kommt dem Land als Wohnraum eine Bedeutung zu, die geprägt ist von der Vorstellungswelt der Stadtbewohner und die viel über deren Sehnsucht aussagt, jedoch wenig Rückschlüsse auf das tatsächliche Landleben zulässt. Mit anderen Worten: Auf dem Land zu wohnen, ist mehr Sehnsucht als Wirklichkeit.

Nüchtern betrachtet ist der Alltag auf dem Land heute dem in der Stadt recht ähnlich. Auch die Landbevölkerung muss morgens zur Arbeit und kommt abends nach Hause. Fernsehen, Handy und Internet sind so präsent wie überall – das Angebot zum Konsum unterscheidet nicht zwischen Wohnorten. Alltagserscheinungen wie der Verkehr können im ländlichen Raum ebenso lästig ausfallen wie in urbanen Zentren. Letztlich haben sich beide Bereiche in den letzten Jahrzehnten stark angenähert. Während das Land in vielen Aspekten »städtischer« wurde, entwickelten sich Städte mehr und mehr zu Orten, in denen es Zonen gibt, die mit dem Landleben assoziiert sind. Phänomene wie Nachbarschaftsgärten, »urban gardening« oder Guerilla-Gärten bringen ein Stück Natur in den Alltag der Städter. Sie pflanzen Tomaten und Karotten in Hochbeeten, ernten gemeinsam mit Nachbarn und tauschen sich über Erfahrungen des ökologischen Landbaus aus. In Megacities wie New York verwandelten sich in den letzten Jahrzehnten ungenutzte Hochhausdächer zu Oasen der ländlichen Tierhaltung. Gewiefte Hobbyfarmer kommen zusammen, um sich nach Büroschluss ihren Ziegen, Hühnern oder anderen Nutztieren zu widmen. Bald jede Großstadt und manchmal sogar jedes Stadtviertel hat heute seinen eigenen Honig. Großstadtimker stellen Bienenstöcke in Parks und Hinterhöfen auf. Die Grenzen zwischen urbanem Raum und Land verschwimmen immer mehr. Die Vorstellung des Lebens auf dem Land jedoch ist davon nicht betroffen, sondern eine Konsequenz wachsender Städte und Sehnsüchte. Letztlich also ist das Wohnen in der Natur eine wirkungsvolle Projektionsfläche für Träume, die Alternativen zum Stadtleben sein wollen und auf unterschiedliche Weise wahr werden können – mal in Form von kleinen urbanen Utopien, mal als gebautes Traumhaus in der Natur.

DIE AVANTGARDE WOHNT AUF DEM LAND

In der modernen Architektur gibt es berühmte historische Beispiele für die Sehnsucht der Städter nach dem Land. So konzipierten Le Corbusier und sein Vetter Pierre Jeanneret die *Villa Savoy* in Poissy westlich von Paris als Wochenenddomizil, dessen Architektur die Natur erfahrbar macht. Inmitten einer großen Wiese inszenieren die Innenräume der Villa den Blick auf die Laubbäume der Umgebung. Ähnlich einer Landschaft, die durchschritten wird, verbindet eine Rampe die einzelnen Etagen und führt bis auf das Dach. Dort endet die »promenade architecturale« auf einer windgeschützten Sonnenterrasse, die die Natur zu einer unmittelbaren Erfahrung werden lässt. Ähnlich vielschichtig fasste Robert Mallet-Stevens in den 1920er-Jahren das Landschaftserlebnis in der Architektur der *Villa Noailles* an der Mittelmeerküste Südfrankreichs. Die mediterrane Winterresidenz für das Ehepaar Charles und Marie-Laure de Noailles ist in ihrem Raumprogramm mit Schwimmhalle, Gymnastik- und Squash-Raum auf Erholung und Freizeit ausgerichtet, wobei die Natur mit zum architektonischen Konzept gehört. Große Pinien umgeben das Haus. Seine Terrassenarchitektur lenkt den Blick auf das Meer und die Bucht von Hyères. In ihrer extravaganten Residenz empfingen die Noailles Freunde und Künstler wie Alberto Giacometti, Francis Poulenc, Salvador Dalí und Luis Buñuel. Fern von Paris, in der mediterranen Landschaft fand die Avantgarde ein Zuhause.

Als der Warenhausbesitzer Edgar J. Kaufmann aus Pittsburgh Frank Lloyd Wright in den 1930er-Jahren mit einem Haus für die Sommerfrische beauftragte, war sein Wunsch ein Zufluchtsort in der Natur der Allegheny Mountains. Frank Lloyd Wright platzierte *Fallingwater* über dem Wasserfall, das Haus breitet sich in verschiedenen Plattformen aus und nutzt die Felsen des Grundstücks als Wände. »Ich möchte, dass Sie mit dem Wasserfall leben, nicht, dass Sie ihn bloß anschauen.

Never has the longing for nature been greater than today – as ever more people live in urban environments. Regarded as an intact place for recreation, the primal nature of the countryside offers an ideal setting for the inner self to find respite from city stress and become peaceful. Living in the countryside – even only at the weekends or during holidays – is the dream of many city dwellers. The more they fit into everyday city life, the greater is their yearning for an alternative. The countryside as a place to live hence obtains a significance that is charged with the imagination of the inhabitants of cities – one that says a lot about their longing, but very little about real country life. In other words: living in the country is more of a nostalgic wish than a reality.

As such, everyday life in the country is rather similar to everyday life in the city. The rural population also goes to work in the morning and comes back in the evening. TV, mobile phones and the web are as ubiquitous as everywhere else – opportunities to consume do not differentiate between where people live. Everyday manifestations like traffic can be just as tedious in rural settings as in urban centres. The two regions have, after all, started to approximate to each other significantly during the past decades. While many aspects of country life have become more "urban", cities have increasingly evolved into places incorporating areas associated with country living. Phenomena such as neighbourhood gardening (using temporarily available space), urban gardening or guerrilla gardening bring a little nature into the lives of city dwellers. They plant tomatoes and carrots in raised beds, harvest with the neighbours and exchange organic farming experiences. Over the last decades, unused roofs of high-rise buildings in megacities like New York have been turned into oases for keeping animals. Smart hobby farmers get together to look after their goats, chicken or other useful animals after office hours. Almost every city, and sometimes even every district, has its own honey nowadays: urban beekeepers set up beehives in parks and backyards.

The boundaries between urban and rural space are becoming fuzzier. This has not, however, had an effect on the image people have of living in the country, which is more a consequence of expanding cities and greater yearning. Living in nature finally lends itself excellently to the projection of dreams that want to be alternatives to city life and come true in different ways – be it in the form of small urban utopias or as a dream house built in nature.

THE AVANT-GARDE LIVES IN THE COUNTRY

Modern architecture is full of famous historical examples illustrating the longing of city dwellers for the countryside. Le Corbusier and his cousin Pierre Jeanneret, for instance, designed the *Villa Savoy* in Poissy to the west of Paris as a weekend house with an architecture in harmony with nature. Situated in the middle of a large meadow, a view of the nearby deciduous trees is offered from the interior of the villa. Calling to mind a walk through the landscape, a ramp connects the individual storeys and leads to the roof. This is where the "promenade architecturale" ends: on a wind-sheltered sun terrace right in the midst of nature.

A similarly multi-layered experience of nature is facilitated by the architecture of the *Villa Noailles* on the coast of southern France designed by Robert Mallet-Stevens in the 1920s. The layout of the Mediterranean winter residence for the couple Charles and Marie-Laure de Noailles is focused on recreation and leisure with an indoor swimming pool, gymnastics and squash room, while nature is part of the architectural concept. Large pine trees surround the house; its terrace architecture leads the eye to the sea and the bay of Hyères. The Noailles liked to receive friends and artists such as Alberto Giacometti, Francis Poulenc, Salvador Dalí and Luis Buñuel in their extravagant house. Far from Paris, the avantgarde of the time found a home in the Mediterranean landscape.

When the department store owner Edgar J. Kaufmann from Pittsburgh asked Frank Lloyd Wright to design a summer holiday home for him in the 1930s, he wanted to find refuge in the nature of the Allegheny Mountains. Frank Lloyd Wright placed *Fallingwater* above a waterfall, with the house spread across various platforms and using rocks located on the site as walls. "I want you to live with the waterfall, not just to look at it, but for it to become an integral part of your lives," the architect explained his approach to Kaufmann. The symbiosis between architecture and nature is

Er soll Bestandteil Ihres Lebens werden«, resümierte der Architekt seinen Ansatz dem Bauherrn gegenüber. Die Symbiose zwischen Architektur und Natur ist bei *Fallingwater* nicht nur für die Raumkonzeption entscheidend, sondern auch für die Materialien, welche die Grenzen zwischen innen und außen obsolet machen.
In der Zielsetzung vergleichbar und doch mit ganz anderen Mitteln umgesetzt, zeigt sich das *Farnsworth House* von Ludwig Mies van der Rohe. 1950/51 bei Plano, Illinois, für Edith Farnsworth als Wochenendhaus errichtet, setzt die Architektur den Gedanken der Nähe zur Natur auf radikale Weise um. Der 140 Quadratmeter große Innenraum des Hauses öffnet sich auf allen Seiten mit raumhohen Glasfassaden zu dem umliegenden Wiesengrundstück. Die transparente Außenhülle verbindet Innen- und Außenraum zu einer Einheit. Aus dem Wohnhaus in der Natur wird hier bewohnte Natur. »Das Haus ist durchsichtig wie ein Röntgenbild«, beschwerte sich die Bauherrin über die konsequente Reduktion ihres Wochenenddomizils, das die Vorteile der Glasfassade für sein kompromissloses architektonisches Konzept nutzte.

DIE RADIKALISIERTE NATURERFAHRUNG

Wenn Architekten heute Rückzugsräume im Grünen entwerfen, so können sie an eine lange Tradition der Architekturgeschichte der Moderne anknüpfen. Gleichwohl ist die Bauaufgabe, einen Wohnsitz auf dem Land zu konzipieren, heute komplexer. Denn in Zeiten der Stadtflucht hat sich das Verlangen nach Natur radikalisiert und will entsprechend gestillt werden. Architektur muss einerseits eine besondere, gesteigerte Naturerfahrung inszenieren und andererseits möglichst einfach erreichbar sein für Besucher aus der Stadt. Das bedeutet, dass das Wohnen in der Natur umso interessanter wird, je besser die entsprechenden Häuser mit ausgebauten Straßen oder Flughäfen in der unmittelbaren Nähe erschlossen sind.
Der französische Entwickler und Galerist Christian Bourdais hat diesen Widerspruch für sich gelöst. Sein Projekt der *Solo Houses*, das er seit 2010 am Rande des Nationalparks bei Barcelona verfolgt, knüpft an die Tradition der Avantgarde an und radikalisiert diese gleichzeitig. Zwei der insgesamt 15 Ferienhäuser, die auf dem 100 Hektar großen Grundstück im katalanischen Gebirgszug Matarrañas gebaut und an Feriengäste vermietet werden sollen, sind bereits fertiggestellt.
Die Architekten Pezo von Ellrichshausen aus Chile und Office Kersten Geers David Van Severen aus Belgien erhielten jeweils »cartes blanches«, um ihre Architektur jenseits gängiger Typologien und Einschränkungen umzusetzen.
Geers und Van Severen entwarfen ihr außergewöhnliches Landhaus als einen Ring mit 40 Metern Durchmesser, der sich zwischen die Olivenbäume und die kargen Wälder der Umgebung schiebt. Es gibt kein Vorne und Hinten. Alle Fassaden sind gleich. Der Blick durch das Fenster ist im digitalen Zeitalter zur 360-Grad-Erfahrung gesteigert, die den Innenraum immer und überall mit dem Außenraum verquickt. Durch Glasfassaden, die alle vier abgeschlossenen Gebäudesegmente des Hauses wie ein Vorhang umrunden, wird das Landschaftserlebnis unmittelbar. Im Flachdach des *Solo House II* ist die technische Ausstattung untergebracht – neben den Wassertanks sind dies auch Photovoltaikelemente und Generatoren. Die ungewöhnliche Wohnidee von Geers und Van Severen hinterfragt sämtliche Konventionen. Das Haus zeigt sich als Showcase einer radikalisierten Naturerfahrung für Städter, die in ihren Ferien das Landschaftserlebnis suchen und dabei nicht auf Annehmlichkeiten wie einen Pool verzichten wollen.
Ähnlich stringent inszeniert das *Tree Hotel* in Schweden die Natur. Als »landscape hotel where nature and imagination run wild« heißt das gewagte Unternehmen in den Wäldern Lapplands – etwa eine Flugstunde von Stockholm entfernt – seine Gäste willkommen.
Alle Hotelzimmer sind von skandinavischen Architekten konzipiert und als einzelne Behausungen in den Wald gebaut. Das norwegische Architekturbüro Snøhetta entwickelte als jüngsten Neuzugang des Projekts ein Baumhaus mit 100 Quadratmetern Fläche, das 10 Meter über dem Boden zwischen den Wipfeln der Kiefern schwebt. Die Außenhülle aus schwarz verkohltem Holz der Region bettet das Baumhaus in seine Umgebung ein. Auf seiner Unterseite ist eine 1:1-Fotografie mit einer Aufnahme der Bäume vor dem Bauzustand angebracht – das Camouflage-Spiel der Architektur wird auf diese Weise noch sublimiert.

not only decisive for *Fallingwater's* spatial layout, but also for the materials making the borders between inside and outside obsolete.
Comparable in terms of objective, but realised using entirely different means, is *Farnsworth House* designed by Ludwig Mies van der Rohe. Built as a weekend house for Edith Farnsworth near Plano, Illinois, in 1950/51, the architecture implements the idea of closeness to nature in a radical way. Room-high glass facades on all sides open up the 140-square-metres interior of the house to the surrounding meadowland. Inside and outside space become one through the transparent outer envelope. The house in nature allows living with nature. "The house is transparent, like an X-ray," Edith Farnsworth noted about the radical reduction of her weekend domicile, which made use of the advantages of glass facades for its uncompromising architecture.

RADICALISED EXPERIENCE OF NATURE

When architects design places to retreat to amid nature, they can continue in a long tradition of modern architectural history. The task of designing a country home has, however, become more complicated nowadays. In these times of urban flight, the longing for nature has become radicalised and wants to be satisfied accordingly. Architecture has to offer a special, remarkable experience of nature on the one hand, while also being easily accessible to visitors from the city on the other. This means that the greater the accessibility of such houses with regard to proper roads or a nearby airport, the more interesting living in nature will become. The French property developer and gallery owner Christian Bourdais has found an individual solution to this contradiction. His *Solo Houses* project at the edge of the National Park near Barcelona, which he has worked on since 2010, continues as well as radicalises the tradition of the avant-garde. Two of a total of fifteen vacation homes to be built on an area of 100 hectares in the mountainous Matarrañas region in Catalunya and rented to holiday guests are already completed. The architects Pezo von Ellrichshausen from Chile and Office Kersten Geers David Van Severen from Belgium were each given carte blanche to realise their architecture beyond customary typologies and limitations.
Geers and Van Severen designed their extraordinary country house as a ring with a diameter of 40 metres, placed between olive trees and the sparse forestation in the area. There is no front and no back. All facades are identical. The view from the window is a 360-degree panorama experience in line with the digital age we live in, amalgamating interior with exterior always and everywhere. Glass facades, surrounding all four self-contained building segments of the house like a curtain, allow a direct experience of the landscape.
The technical equipment of *Solo House* II, such as water tanks, photovoltaic elements and generators, is accommodated on the flat roof. Geers and Van Severens unusual habitation concept questions all conventions. The house is a showcase of a radicalised experience of nature for city dwellers looking for a landscape experience in their holidays, while not wishing to do without conveniences like a pool.
The focus on nature is similarly pronounced as far as the *Tree Hotel* in Sweden is concerned. The daring venture in the forests of Lapland – about one hour by plane from Stockholm – welcomes its guests to a "landscape hotel where nature and imagination run wild". All hotel rooms were designed by Scandinavian architects and built as single dwellings in the forest. The latest addition to this project is a tree house designed by the Norwegian architectural office Snøhetta, offering an area of 100 square metres amid the tops of pines 10 metres above the ground. The outer shell of charred local timber integrates the tree house into the surroundings. A 1:1 print of a photograph of the trees before building began, fitted to the underside of the tree house, perfects an already effective architectural camouflage.

LANDSCAPE AND ARCHITECTURE OF RESPONSIBILITY

Today, decisive factors for stringent concepts in the design of country residences include topography and landscape, local resources and sophisticated energy concepts. The responsibility of architects to take these parameters into account in their designs, and to find solutions that respect and engage with different natural environments, has increased considerably since historical modernity. The means and concepts with which these objectives can be

LANDSCHAFT UND ARCHITEKTUR DER VERANTWORTUNG

Topografie und Landschaft, lokale Ressourcen und ausgeklügelte Energiekonzepte sind heute entscheidende Faktoren für stringente Wohnkonzepte auf dem Land. Die Verantwortung für Architekten, im Umgang mit diesen Parametern zu entwerfen und Lösungen zu finden, die unterschiedliche Naturräume respektieren und auf sie reagieren, ist seit der historischen Moderne deutlich gestiegen. Mit welchen Mitteln und Konzepten diese Ziele umgesetzt werden können – von der vorfabrizierten Holzhütte im Kaninmassiv in Slowenien bis zur Wohnplattform im brasilianischen Regenwald – zeigen die Beispiele dieses Buchs. Sie verdeutlichen, dass der Landschaftsraum als konstruierte Vorstellungswelt zu Entwürfen beflügelt, die sich radikal auf das Naturerlebnis einlassen und mit der Natur interagieren. Ist die bewohnte Natur ein Sehnsuchtsziel, so ist einer der tragenden Gründe für diese Sehnsucht die wachsende Faszination, die Wertschätzung und der Respekt, der Natur- und Landschaftsräumen heute vielerorts entgegengebracht wird.

realised – from a prefabricated wooden hut in the Kanin Mountains in Slovenia, to a living platform in the Brazilian rain forest – are illustrated in this book. They exemplify that landscape, as a constructed world of the imagination, can inspire designs that permit a radical experience of nature while also engaging with it. If living in nature is something we yearn for, then one of the main reasons for this longing is the growing fascination, appreciation and respect that we have for nature and landscapes today.

Robert Mallet-Stevens konzipierte die *Villa Noailles* in Hyères als Terrassenlandschaft mit mediterranem Garten. Hier verbrachte das Pariser Ehepaar Noailles den Winter – gemeinsam mit Gästen und befreundeten Künstlern.

Robert Mallet-Stevens designed the *Villa Noailles* in Hyères as a terrace landscape with a Mediterranean garden. The Parisian couple, Madame and Monsieur de Noailles, liked to spend the winter here – together with guests and artist friends.

Solo House von Office Kersten Geers David Van Severen: Die ringförmige Struktur liegt mitten in der mediterranen Landschaft südlich von Barcelona. Das radikale Wohnexperiment lässt der Natur den Vortritt und inszeniert sie als außergewöhnliche Qualität.

Solo House by Office Kersten Geers David Van Severen: the ring-shaped structure lies in the middle of the Mediterranean landscape south of Barcelona. The radical housing experiment gives Nature priority and presents it as an exceptional quality.

Solo House von Pezo von Ellrichshausen Architects: Alle Wohnräume des Feriendomizils öffnen sich auf eine umlaufende Loggia, die als Freisitz dient. Von hier schweift der Blick der Gäste über die Berg- und Hügellandschaft in die Ferne.

Solo House by Pezo von Ellrichshausen Architects: all living spaces of the holiday domicile open up to a loggia extending all around the house and also serving as an outdoor sitting area. Guests can enjoy an unobstructed view across the hilly landscape.

Landschaft und Imagination: Das schwedische *Treehotel* wirbt mit besonderen Abenteuern in der Natur. Dazu zählen Nordlichter, Schlittenhundfahrten und Anglertrips. Die einzelnen, innovativen Unterkünfte des Abenteuerhotels sind als Baumhäuser von unterschiedlichen Architekten konzipiert. Oben: *The Ufo* (Inderingsgruppen, 2010), links: *The Blue Cone* (SandelSandberg, 2010), rechts: *The 7th Room* (Snøhetta, 2016).

Landscape and imagination: the Swedish *Treehotel* promises special nature-focussed adventures. These include the Northern Lights, sled dog tours and fishing trips. The adventure hotel offers individual accommodation in tree houses designed by different architects. Top: The Ufo (Inderingsgruppen, 2010), left: The Blue Cone (SandelSandberg, 2010), right: The 7th Room (Snøhetta, 2016).

Projekte

Projects

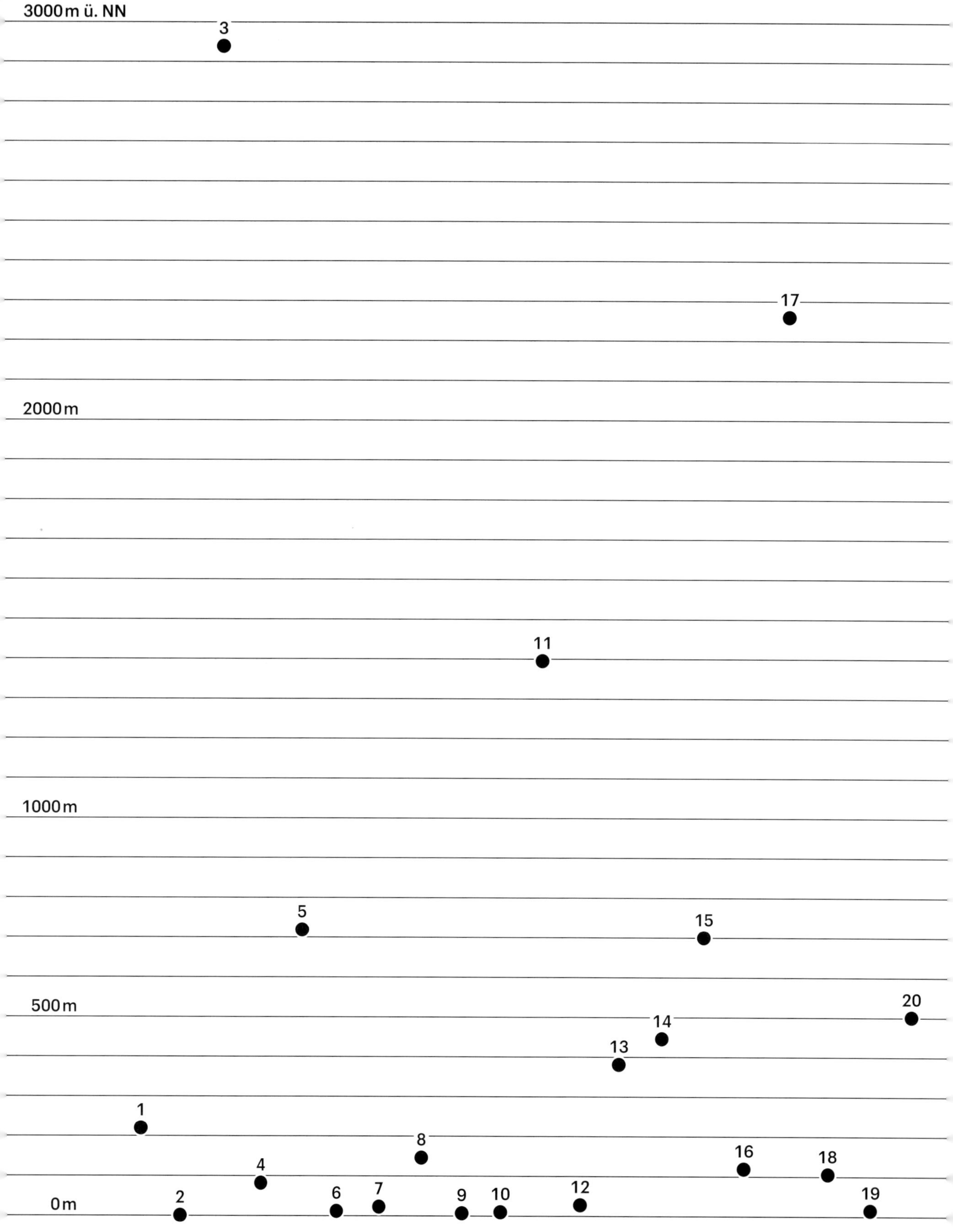

3000 m ü. NN
2000 m
1000 m
500 m
0 m
1
2
3
4
5
6
7
8
9
10
11
12
13
14
15
16
17
18
19
20

Mit Blick über den Lago Maggiore

View across Lake Maggiore

Aus dem schmalen, steilen Grundstück am See erhebt sich turmartig ein Monolith aus vier aufeinandergestapelten Geschossen. Die Architekten nutzten die Topografie des Tessiner Ufers, um Landschaft, Ausblicke und spannungsvolle Raumfolgen zu inszenieren. Die Außenräume – der Eingangshof, zu dem die Treppe von den Autostellplätzen auf dem Dach hinunter führt, sowie der tiefer liegende Wohnhof – sind über Fenstertüren mit den Wohnräumen verbunden. Diese gläsernen Elemente können komplett in der Wand verschwinden, Außen und Innen gehen dann nahtlos ineinander über. Der Wohnhof, in dem zwei Olivenbäume stehen, bildet das Herzstück des Hauses, hier treffen sich die Wege wie auf einem Dorfplatz.

Aufgrund des durchgängig verwendeten gewaschenen Betons verbinden sich Haus und Höfe zu einer Einheit, die sich in den Landschaftsraum integriert. Im Inneren nehmen die verputzten Wände und Decken die raue, unregelmäßige Struktur der Fassaden wieder auf, sodass die Unterschiede zwischen Innen- und Außenraum verwischen.

A monolith composed of four storeys stacked on top of each other rises up like a tower from the steep and narrow plot of land by the lake. The architects made use of the topography of the Ticino lakeside to incorporate the breathtaking landscape and views, as well as create fascinating spatial sequences. The exterior spaces – an entrance area (accessed by stairs from the parking spaces on the roof) and a courtyard used as a living area further down – are connected to the residential spaces through French doors. These glazed elements can fully disappear in the walls, removing the boundary between inside and outside. The courtyard occupied by two olive trees is the core of the house, a place of interaction much like a village square.

The use of washed concrete throughout makes the house and courtyards form a homogeneous unit that is integrated in the surrounding landscape. The rough, irregular structure of the outer facades is echoed by the plastered walls and ceilings within, blurring the differences between inside and outside.

Architekten: Wespi de Meuron Romeo
Bauherr: privat
Tragwerksplaner: Pedrazzini Guidotti Sagl
Bauphysik: IFEC Consulenze SA
Material: Gewaschener Beton
Region/Land: Tessin, Schweiz
Funktion: Ferienhaus
Nutzung: temporär

Architects: Wespi de Meuron Romeo
Client: Private
Structural engineering: Pedrazzini Guidotti Sagl
Building physics: IFEC Consulenze SA
Material: Washed concrete
Region/Country: Ticino, Switzerland
Function: Holiday home
Utilisation: Temporary

Grundrisse / Schnitt
Maßstab 1:250

1 Essen
2 Küche
3 Abstellraum
4 Hof
5 Eingang
6 Keller
7 Wohnen
8 Zimmer
9 Fitnessraum
10 Schlafen
11 Technik
12 Sauna

Floor plans / Section
Scale 1:250

1 Dining room
2 Kitchen
3 Storeroom
4 Courtyard
5 Entrance
6 Cellar
7 Living room
8 Room
9 Gym
10 Bedroom
11 Services
12 Sauna

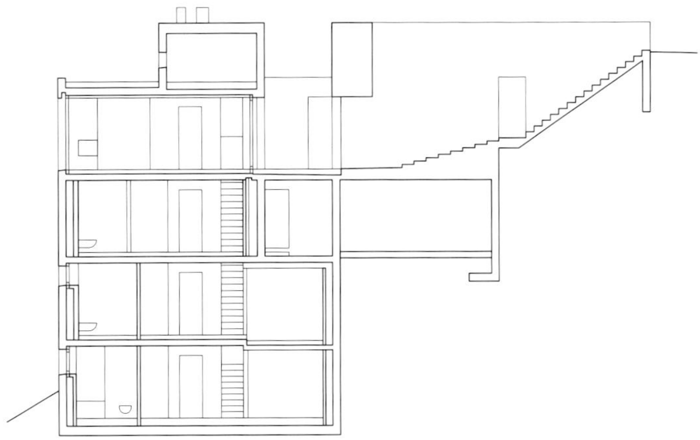

aa

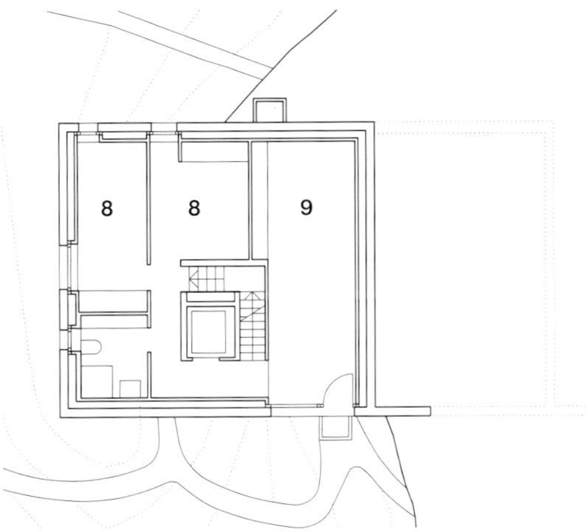

1. Obergeschoss /
First floor

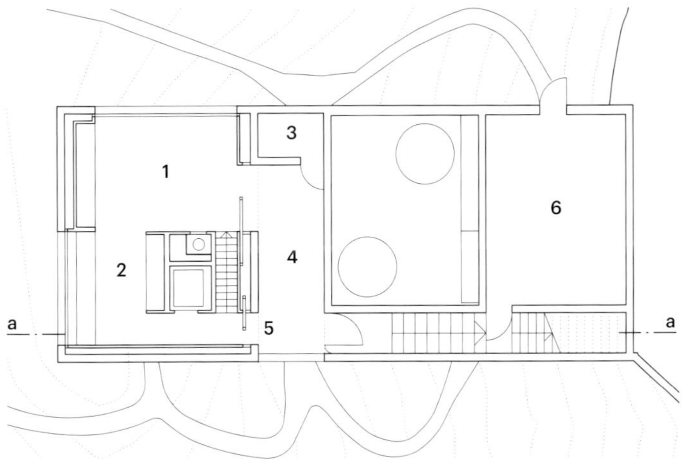

3. Obergeschoss /
Third floor

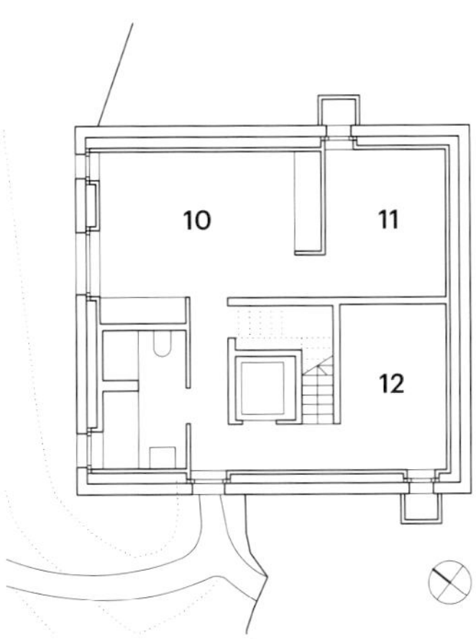

Erdgeschoss /
Ground floor

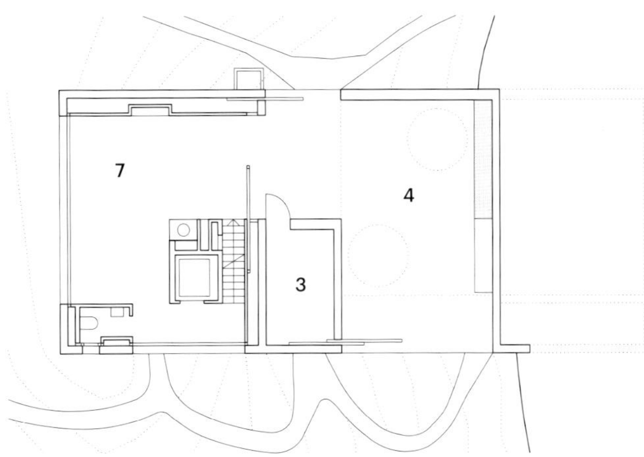

2. Obergeschoss /
Second floor

Dunkler Schattenwurf in Norfolk

Dark shadow cast in Norfolk

In der Fluss- und Seenlandschaft der Norfolk Broads steht eine der letzten windbetriebenen Wasserpumpenmühlen Englands, die Hunsett Mill. Das Cottage neben dem Gebäude bewohnten früher die Mühlenwärter. Im Laufe der Jahre wurde das Wohnhaus durch zahlreiche Anbauten ergänzt. Acme entfernten diese und erweitern das traditionelle Backsteingebäude um einen Flügel, der wie ein Schatten des Bestands wirkt und diesem den Vorrang lässt. Mit vier Giebeln und Fassaden aus schwarz geflämmter Holzverkleidung komplettiert der Neubau das Cottage. Die Technik des Verkohlens, um das Holz widerstandsfähig zu machen, war in der Region früher für landwirtschaftliche Gebäude üblich.
Das Ferienhaus ist in Holztafelbauweise errichtet, in seinem Inneren bilden naturbelassene Oberflächen einen starken Kontrast zum dunklen Äußeren. Geschickt platzierte Fenster, die als rahmenlose Öffnungen in den Fassaden sitzen, fangen schöne Ausblicke ein. Dank einer Solarthermieanlage, Erdwärmepumpe und Biomasseanlage sowie der Verwendung überwiegend nachwachsender Baustoffe erfüllt das Haus im Naturparadies des Nationalparks auch die Kriterien nachhaltigen Bauens.

Architekten: ACME
Bauherr: Catriona and John Dodsworth, Joanna and Jon Emery
Tragwerksplanung: Adams Kara Taylor
Servicetechniker: Hoare Lea
Kostenplaner: Philip Panks & Partners/Cyril Sweett
Nachhaltigkeit: Hoare Lea
Material: Holz, Stein/Ziegel
Region/Land: Norfolk, England, Großbritannien
Funktion: Ferienhaus
Nutzung: temporär

One of the last wind-powered water pumping mills in England – Hunsett Mill – is located in the Norfolk Broads, a landscape characterised by rivers and lakes. The cottage next to the mill used to be a residence for the keeper of the mill and was supplemented by numerous extensions over the years. These were removed by Acme, who chose to add an extension to the traditional brick building, which looks like a shadow of the existing house and clearly respects its seniority. The new extension of the cottage has four gables and its facades are clad with black charred timber. Making wood more resistant to weathering by charring is a technique that was commonly used for agricultural buildings in the region in the past.
The holiday home was built as a frame structure. The exposed natural finish of the internal surfaces creates a stark contrast to the dark exterior. Uplifting views are captured by cleverly positioned windows, placed as frameless openings in the facades. Sustainable building criteria are fulfilled by the cottage situated in the natural paradise of the national park, thanks to utilisation of a solar heating system, a ground source heat pump and a biomass system as well as predominantly renewable building materials.

Architects: ACME
Client: Catriona and John Dodsworth, Joanna and Jon Emery
Structural engineering: Adams Kara Taylor
Services engineer: Hoare Lea
Quantity surveyor: Philip Panks & Partners/Cyril Sweett
Sustainability: Hoare Lea
Material: Timber and brick
Region/Country: Norfolk, England, Great Britain
Function: Holiday home
Utilisation: Temporary

HUNSETT MILL, STALHAM (GB)

aa

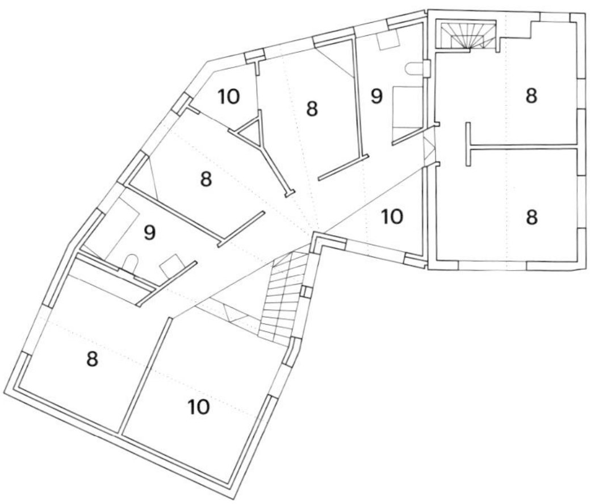

Obergeschoss /
First floor

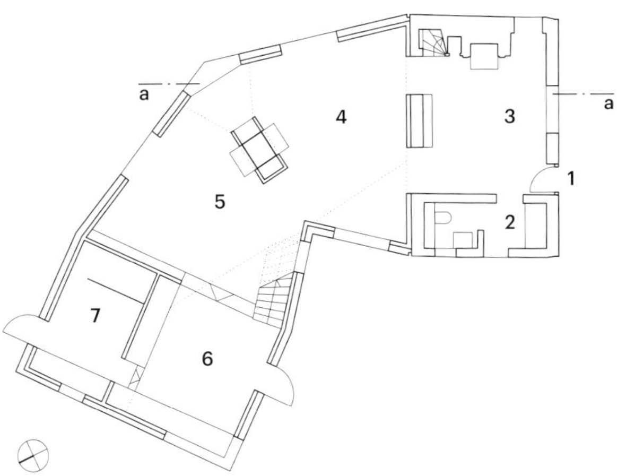

Erdgeschoss /
Ground floor

Grundrisse / Schnitt
Maßstab 1:250

1 Eingang
2 Garderobe
3 Arbeitszimmer
4 Essen
5 Wohnen
6 Küche mit Essplatz
7 Hauswirtschaftsraum / Technik
8 Schlafen
9 Bad
10 Luftraum

Floor plans / Section
Scale 1:250

1 Entrance
2 Dressing room
3 Study
4 Dining room
5 Living room
6 Kitchen with dinette
7 Utility room / Services
8 Bedroom
9 Bathroom
10 Void

Berghütten in den Rocky Mountains

Mountain cabins in the Rocky Mountains

Die Non-Profit-Organisation Outward Bound bietet Naturabenteuer in über 30 Ländern an, unter anderem auch im US-amerikanischen Bundesstaat Colorado. Dort entstanden 2015 in Zusammenarbeit mit dem Colorado Building Workshop der University of Denver 14 ungedämmte Sommerhütten auf 3000 Metern Höhe. Ein Jahr später kamen am Fuß der Gebirgskette Sawatch Range sieben weitere Unterkünfte hinzu, die dank Wärmeschutz ganzjährig bewohnbar sind. Die Studententeams entwarfen die unterschiedlichen Wohnboxen als kostengünstige Strukturen aus widerstandsfähigen Materialien. Dunkle Stahlplatten verkleiden die Fassaden der vorgefertigten Holzkonstruktionen, kombiniert mit natürlich belassenem Holz. Farblich fügen sich die aufgeständerten Behausungen wie selbstverständlich in den Kiefernwald ein. Die Innenräume sind mit Birkensperrholz verkleidet und bieten Platz für ein oder zwei Personen. Speziell entworfene Einbaumöbel bilden die zweckmäßige Einrichtung. Jede Hütte ist in ihrer Ausrichtung individuell an die Topografie angepasst, sodass die Ausblicke von der Veranda in den Wald und auf die Berge der Mosquito Range in der Ferne jeweils unterschiedlich ausfallen.

The international non-profit organisation Outward Bound offers natural adventures in more than 30 countries, including the state of Colorado, in the United States. In collaboration with the Colorado Building Workshop of the University of Colorado Denver, 14 non-insulated summer cabins were built there at an altitude of 3,000 metres in 2015. Seven further huts were added at the foot of the Sawatch Range one year later. Fitted with thermal insulation, these can be used throughout the year. Student teams designed the different box-like dwellings as cost-effective structures made of durable materials. The facades of the prefabricated timber constructions are clad with dark steel sheeting combined with untreated wood. Built on stilts, the lodgings are designed as natural components of the pine forest. The interior spaces are clad with birch plywood and are big enough for one or two persons. Furnishings are functional and consist of specially designed built-in furniture. The orientation of each cabin is individually adapted to the topography, permitting a variety of views of the forest and the Mosquito Range in the distance from each veranda.

Architekten: Colorado Building Workshop
Bauherr: Colorado Outward Bound School
Tragwerksplanung: Andy Paddock, Structuralist
Material: warm gewalztes Stahlblech, Zeder, Birkensperrholz, Stahlrahmen
Region / Land: Colorado, Vereinigte Staaten von Amerika
Funktion: Personalunterkunft
Nutzung: permanent

Architects: Colorado Building Workshop
Client: Colorado Outward Bound School
Structural engineering: Andy Paddock, Structuralist
Material: Hot rolled steel, cedar, birch plywood, steel frame
Region / Country: Colorado, United States of America
Function: Staff housing
Utilisation: Permanent

Grundrisse / Schnitt
Maßstab 1:100

1 Bett mit Stauraum
2 Schreibtisch
3 Einbauregal
4 Veranda
5 Bank

Floor plans / Section
Scale 1:100

1 Bed with storage
2 Desk
3 Fitted shelving
4 Veranda
5 Bench

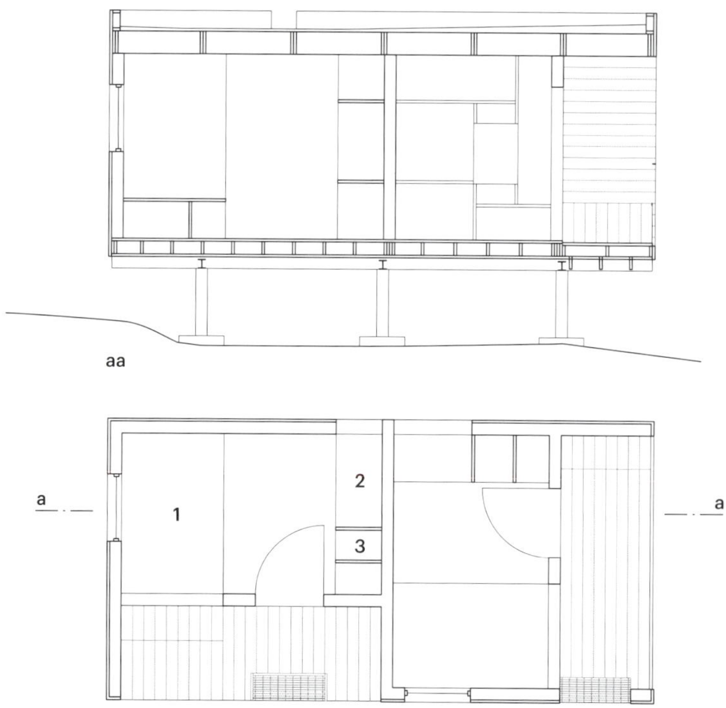

Hütte T /
Cabin T

MIKROHÜTTEN, LEADVILLE, COLORADO (US)

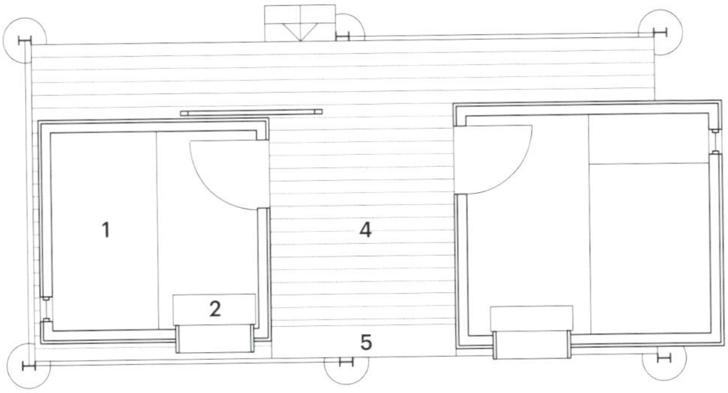

Hütte A /
Cabin A

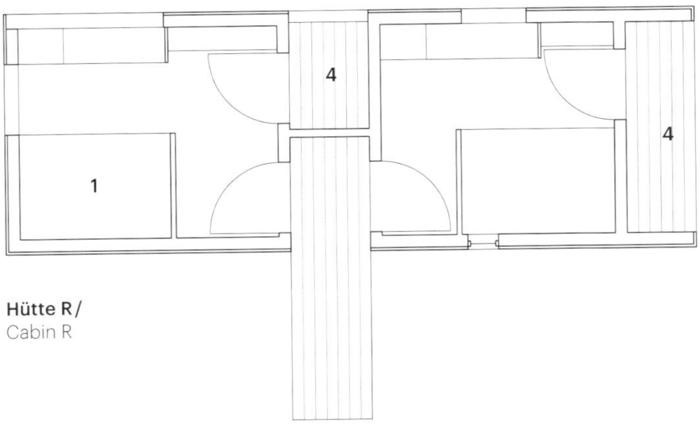

Hütte R /
Cabin R

Turm-Ensemble in der Île-de-France

Tower ensemble in Île-de-France

Auf den ersten Blick fallen von dem Anbau an eine Orangerie aus dem 18. Jahrhundert nur die fünf Betontürme ins Auge – sie ragen über den umliegenden alten Baumbestand hinaus. Doch bei genauerem Betrachten erschließt sich, wie kunstvoll die Architekten den Neubau für eine Familie mit vier Kindern in die malerische Landschaft der westlichen Île-de-France eingebettet haben: Sie gruben das Sockelgeschoss über zwei Meter tief in die Topografie ein und gaben ihm das Aussehen einer bewachsenen Aufschüttung. Nur auf der Gartenseite Richtung Südosten öffnet sich das etwa 50 Meter lange, amorph geformte Erdgeschoss mit raumhohen Verglasungen, die in geschwungenen Natursteinmauern sitzen, zur Landschaft. Genutzt wird dieser Sockelbereich als gemeinschaftliche Wohnfläche der Familie. Fünf turmartige Baukörper durchstoßen das Gründach darüber und bieten den Bewohnern je eine Ankleide, ein eigenes Bad und auf der obersten Ebene das Schlafzimmer. Der Elternturm verfügt zudem über eine Dachterrasse, von der der Blick bis zur Skyline des Pariser Geschäftsviertels La Défense reicht.

Projecting above the old trees on the grounds, only five concrete towers of the extension of an 18th-century orangery catch the eye at first sight. On closer examination, it becomes apparent how sensitively the architects have embedded the new construction, designed for a family with four children, in the picturesque landscape of western Île-de-France. The semi-basement storey was placed up to two metres below the topography and made to look like a vegetated mound of earth. This approximately 50-metres-long, amorphously shaped storey solely opens up towards the garden landscape to the south-east, with room-high glazing placed in curved natural stone walls. The semi-basement area is used as the common living space of the family. Five tower-like structures penetrate the green roof above and offer the residents a private dressing room, a bathroom and, at the very top, a bedroom. The parents' tower also features a roof terrace with a view extending to the skyline of the Parisian business district La Défense.

Architekten: christian pottgiesser architecturespossibles
Bauherr: privat
Material: Ortbeton, Natursteinmauerwerk, Metall- und Holzrahmenverglasungen
Region / Land: Yvelines, Île-de-France, Frankreich
Funktion: Wohnhaus
Nutzung: permanent

Architects: christian pottgiesser architecturespossibles
Client: Private
Material: In-situ concrete, natural stone masonry, metal- and timber-framed glazing
Region / Country: Yvelines, Île-de-France, France
Function: Residential home
Utilisation: Permanent

Grundrisse / Schnitt
Maßstab 1:400

1 Bestand Orangerie
2 Zugang Bestand
3 Eingang
4 gemeinschaftlich genutzte Wohnfläche
5 Terrasse
6 Ankleide
7 Bad
8 Schlafzimmer
9 Dachterrasse

Floor plans / Section
Scale 1:400

1 Existing orangery
2 Access to existing structure
3 Entrance
4 General living area
5 Terrace
6 Dressing room
7 Bathroom
8 Bedroom
9 Roof terrace

 MAISON L, ÎLE-DE-FRANCE (FR)

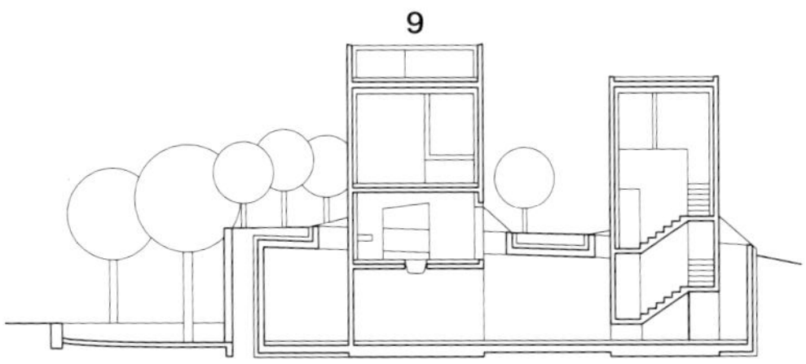

aa

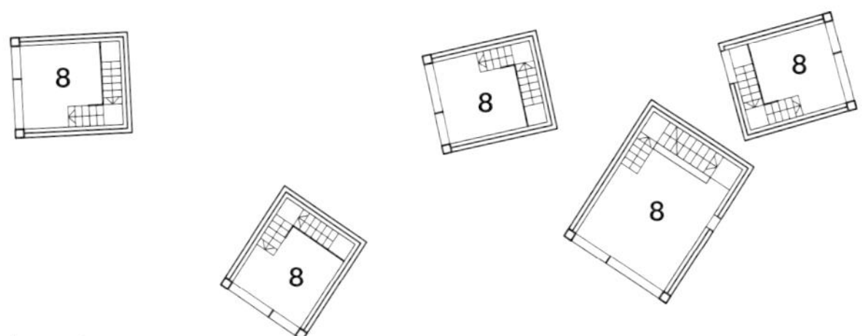

2. Obergeschoss/
Second floor

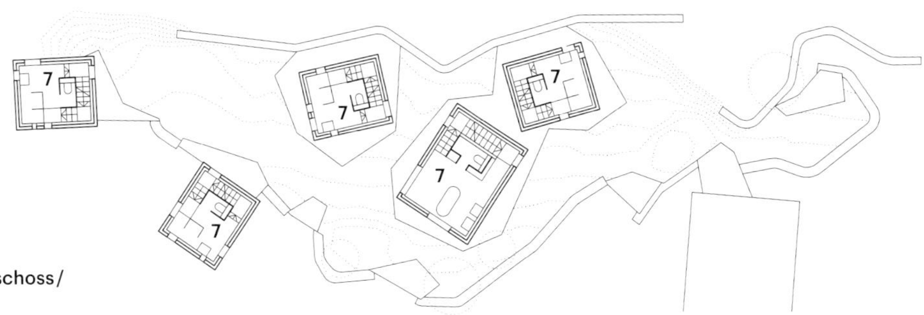

1. Obergeschoss/
First floor

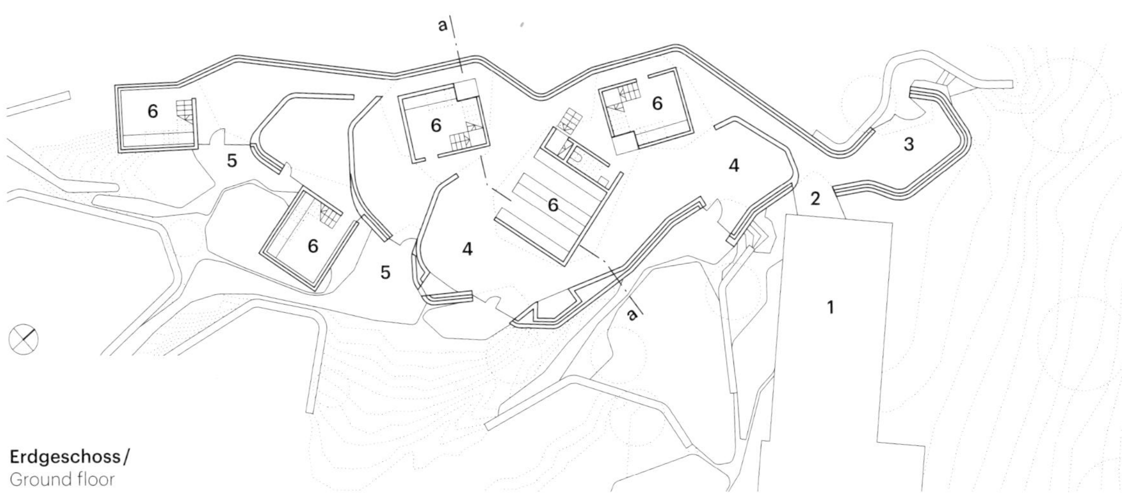

Erdgeschoss/
Ground floor

Satteldachhaus im Bregenzerwald

Gable roof house in Bregenz Forest

Das Motiv eines Baumstamms liegt dem lang gestreckten Wohnhaus auf einer schattigen Streuwiese am Ortsrand zugrunde. Mit seiner holzverschalten Fassade vermittelt das Satteldachgebäude zwischen dem angrenzenden Mischwald und dem Siedlungsgebiet. Als Reverenz an traditionelle landwirtschaftliche Bauten im Bregenzerwald teilt eine Tenne das Haus in einen Wohn- und einen Arbeitsbereich. Die geschützte Zwischenzone mit raumhohen Schiebetoren wird mal als Innenraumerweiterung und mal als Freiraum mit angeschlossener Terrasse genutzt. Außerdem bildet sie das Entree für den Wohnbereich und das Atelier.

Im Inneren sind die Räume vollständig mit Holz verkleidet. Im Kontrast dazu stehen die eingestellten Raumzellen mit schwarz gefärbten Sichtbetonoberflächen, die Bad, Speisekammer und Treppe aufnehmen. Der Großteil des verwendeten Holzes wurde im eigenen Wald geschlagen, insgesamt kamen 70 Tannen und Fichten zum Einsatz – und zwar so, dass jeweils die vollständigen Bäume verwendet werden konnten.

The long shape of the residential building is reminiscent of a tree trunk lying on a shady meadow used to grow hay for bedding situated on the outskirts of the village. With a timber-clad facade, the gable roof building mediates between an adjacent mixed forest and a housing development area. As a reference to traditional farming buildings in Bregenz Forest, a threshing floor divides the house into a residential and working area.

The sheltered intermediate space with room-high sliding doors may be used to extend the interior or alternatively be converted to an outdoor space with an adjoining terrace, as required. It also forms the entrance to the living area and the studio.

Inside, the rooms are fully clad with wood. This contrasts with the blackened, exposed-concrete surfaces of the units containing the bathroom, pantry and stairs. Most of the timber used was obtained from the client's own privately owned forest. The 70 fir and spruce trees needed in total were utilised entirely.

Architekten: Bernardo Bader Architekten
Bauherr: privat
Tragwerksplanung: Plan 3
Haustechnik: Siegfried Steurer Installationen Energietechnik
Material: Sichtbeton, Kupferblech (Dach), heimische Hölzer Tanne, Fichte, Lärche, Ulme (Holzelementbau + Innenausbau), Lehmziegel
Region / Land: Vorarlberg, Österreich
Funktion: Wohnhaus mit Studio
Nutzung: permanent

Architects: Bernardo Bader Architekten
Client: Private
Structural engineering: Plan 3
HVAC: Siegfried Steurer Installationen Energietechnik
Material: Concrete, copper sheet (Roof), local timber: fir, spruce, larch, elm (construction using timber elements + interior finishing), loam blocks
Region / Country: Vorarlberg, Austria
Function: Residence with studio
Utilisation: Permanent

Grundrisse / Schnitte
Maßstab 1:400

1 Wohnzimmer
2 Küche / Esszimmer
3 Lagerraum
4 Eingang / Garderobe
5 überdachter Freibereich / Tenne
6 Büro
7 Garage
8 Luftraum
9 Schlafzimmer
10 Wäscheabwurf
11 Terrasse
12 Zimmer
13 Galerie
14 Dachboden

Floor plans / Sections
Scale 1:400

1 Living room
2 Kitchen / Dining
3 Store
4 Entrance / cloakroom
5 Covered open space / "threshing floor"
6 Office
7 Garage
8 Void
9 Bedroom
10 Laundry chute
11 Terrace
12 Room
13 Loft
14 Attic

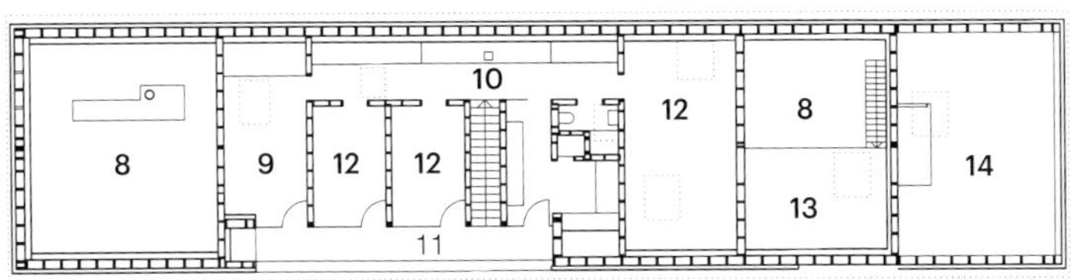

Obergeschoss /
First floor

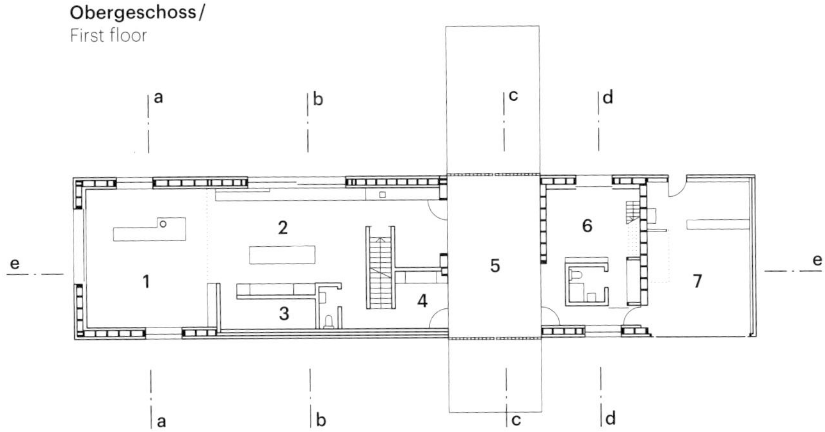

Erdgeschoss /
Ground floor

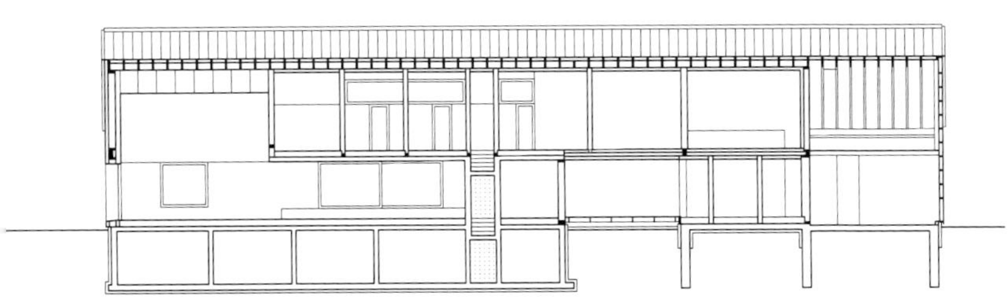

ee

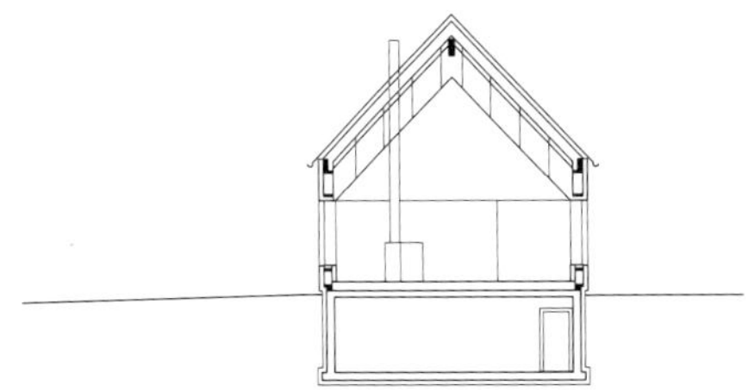

aa

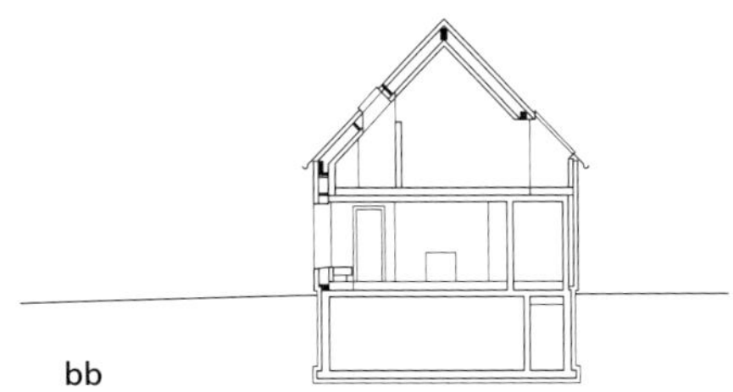

bb

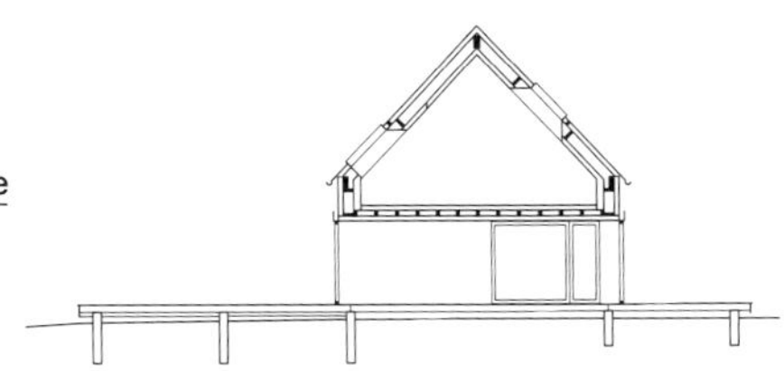

cc

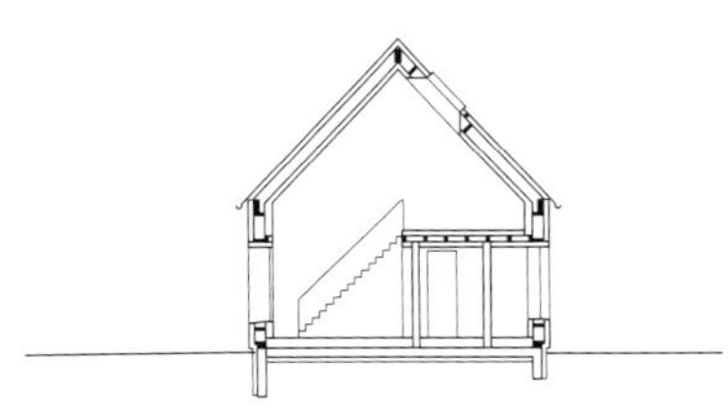

dd

Auf Kufen am Coromandel-Strand

On runners on Coromandel beach

Dass diese Ferienunterkunft an einem der Traumstrände Neuseelands auf Kufen steht, hat einen guten Grund: Sie liegt in einer ausgewiesenen Erosionszone und muss daher demontierbar sein. Die Architekten entwarfen einen mobilen Bau, der sich mit einem Traktor bewegen lässt. Geschlossen fügt sich die Box mit ihrer rauen Holzfassade unauffällig in die Dünenlandschaft ein und ist gegen Wind und Wetter geschützt. Kurbeln die Bewohner, eine fünfköpfige Familie, den großen Klappladen an der Front nach oben, so öffnet sich der zweigeschossige Wohnraum hinter der Glasfassade auf den Südpazifik. Das nur 40 Quadratmeter umfassende Innere ist einfach und funktional und nutzt den verfügbaren Platz optimal aus. Im Erdgeschoss liegt die gemeinschaftliche Familienzone, das Elternbett steht auf der Galerie, während die Kinder im dreistöckigen Etagenbett im rückwärtigen Anbau schlafen.
Der hochgefahrene Laden bildet ein Vordach, der den Innenraum im Sommer vor Hitze schützt, die flachere Sonnenstrahlung im Winter aber einfallen lässt. Stahltonnen fangen das Regenwasser für die Nutzung in Dusche und Toilette auf, für das Abwasser ist eine biologische Kleinkläranlage installiert. Trinkwasser- und Stromversorgung erfolgen über das öffentliche Netz.

There is a good reason why this holiday retreat on one of New Zealand's idyllic beaches stands on a sled structure: it lies within a coastal erosion zone where all of the buildings must be removable. The architects designed a mobile structure that can be moved with a tractor. The closed box with a rough timber facade fits unobtrusively into the dune landscape and is protected against wind and weather. When the owners – a family of five – winch open the large shutter at the front, the glass-fronted two-storey living space opens up to the South Pacific. The design of the 40-square-metres within is simple and functional, with optimal utilisation of available space. A common family area is located on the ground floor, with a lofted sleeping zone for the parental bed, while the children have a triple bunk bed in an extension at the back.
The raised shutter forms an awning, protecting the interior from the heat in summer, while admitting light from the lower winter sun. Steel drums catch rain water for use in the shower and toilet; a biological waste water treatment system is installed. Potable water and electricity are supplied by the public grid.

Architekten: Crosson Architects
Bauherr: privat
Material: Holz, Stahl
Region / Land: Coromandel, Neuseeland
Funktion: Ferienhaus
Nutzung: temporär

Architects: Crosson Architects
Client: Private
Material: Timber, steel
Region / Country: Coromandel, New Zealand
Function: Holiday home
Utilisation: Temporary

Grundrisse / Schnitte
Maßstab 1:200

1 Wohnen
2 Essen
3 Küche
4 Leiter
5 Bad
6 Etagenbetten
7 Schlafgalerie

Floor plans / Sections
Scale 1:200

1 Living room
2 Dining room
3 Kitchen
4 Ladder
5 Bathroom
6 Bunk bedroom
7 Sleeping loft

HÜTTE AUF KUFEN, WHANGAPOUA (NZ)

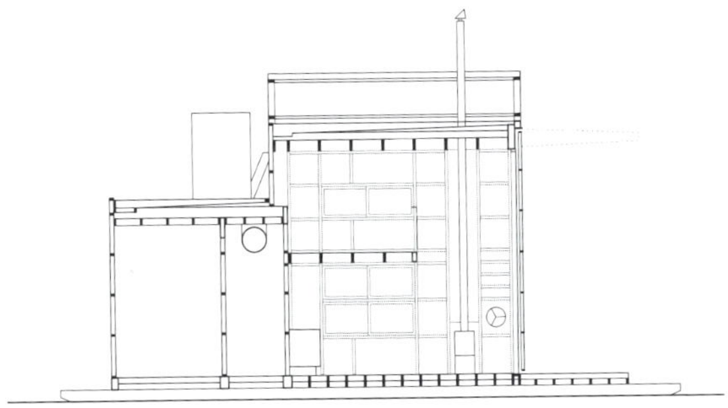

aa

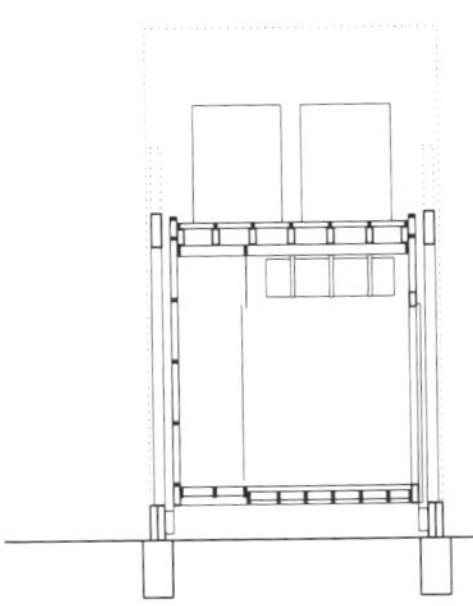

bb

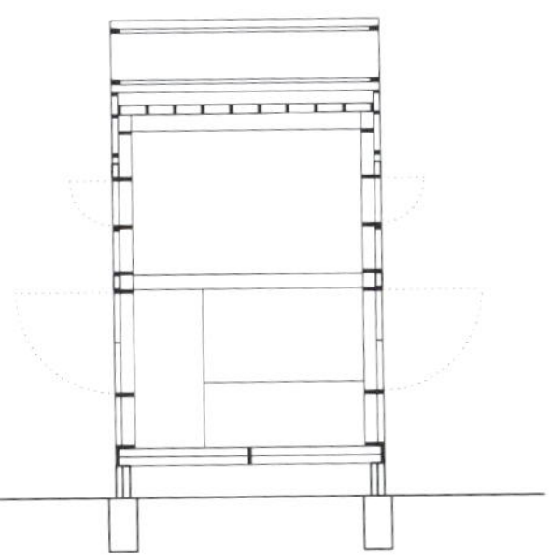

cc

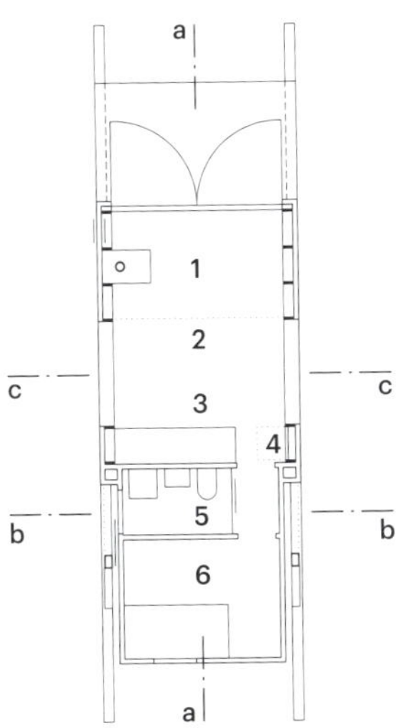

Erdgeschoss / Ground floor

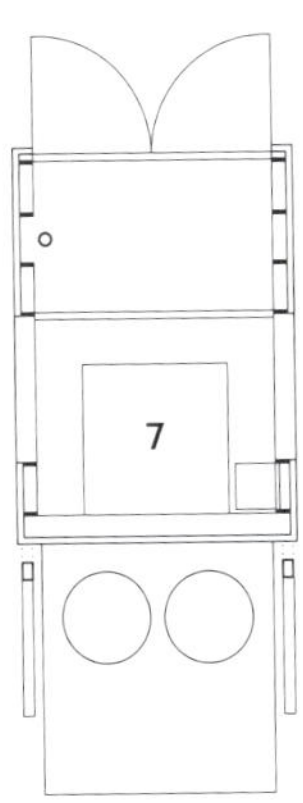

Obergeschoss / First floor

Auf dem Felsgrund der Schären

On the rocks of Stockholm's archipelago

Karge Vegetation, Granitfelsen und farbige Holzhäuschen prägen die Insel Lagnö im Stockholmer Schärengarten. Entgegen der lokalen Tradition entschieden sich die Architekten beim Baumaterial des Sommerhauses für Beton, der das Gebäude aus dem felsigen Grund wachsen lässt.
Die witterungsbeständigen Fassaden kommen dem Wunsch des Bauherrn nach einem Haus mit geringem Aufwand für die Instandhaltung entgegen. In den zwei Baukörpern mit vier unterschiedlich hohen Satteldächern sind die Wohn- und Schlafbereiche sowie ein Gästeatelier untergebracht. Verbunden werden die Volumen über eine ebenfalls satteldachförmig ausgebildete Stahl-Glaskonstruktion, die auch als Eingangsbereich dient und den Blick auf die Insellandschaft rahmt. Die schieferbeschichteten Dachbahnen auf den anderen Dächern unterstreichen im Zusammenspiel mit dem Grau der Fassaden das monolithische Erscheinungsbild. Im Inneren bilden warme Holztöne einen Kontrast zum rauen Äußeren. Der Wohnraum öffnet sich über eine große Fensterfront mit Schiebetüren komplett nach draußen, während die an der Rückseite des Hauses liegenden Schlafzimmer introvertierter sind und nur über Dachfenster Licht erhalten.

Architekten: Tham & Videgård Arkitekter
Bauherr: privat
Fachplaner: Sweco, Mathias Karlsson
Material: Ortbeton
Region / Land: Stockholmer Schärengarten, Schweden
Funktion: Ferienhaus
Nutzung: permanent

Sparse vegetation, granite rocks and colourful wooden houses characterise the island of Lagnö located in Stockholm's archipelago, or "skärgård". Contrary to local tradition, the architects of this summer home chose to use concrete as the building material, allowing the construction to grow out of the rocky ground. Weather-resistant facades are in line with the client's specification to design a house requiring little maintenance. The two structures with four gable roofs of different heights accommodate living and sleeping areas as well as a guest studio. The volumes are connected via a steel-glass construction with a similar double-pitched-roof shape that also serves as an entrance area as well as framing the view of the island landscape. In combination with the grey colour of the facades, the slate-covered roofing underlines the monolithic appearance of the structure. Warm wood tones in the interior form a contrast to the rough exterior. A large window front fitted with sliding doors opens up the living space fully, while the bedrooms situated at the back of the house are more introverted and only illuminated through roof windows.

Architects: Tham & Videgård Arkitekter
Client: Private
Structural engineering: Sweco, Mathias Karlsson
Material: In-situ cast concrete
Region / Country: Stockholm archipelago, Sweden
Function: Holiday home
Utilisation: Permanent

Grundriss / Schnitt
Maßstab 1:250

1 Gast/Atelier
2 Pergola
3 Eingang
4 Küche
5 Schlafraum
6 Wohnen/Essen
7 Schwimmbecken

Floor plan / Section
Scale 1:250

1 Guest/Atelier
2 Pergola
3 Entrance
4 Kitchen
5 Bedroom
6 Living/Dining
7 Swimming pool

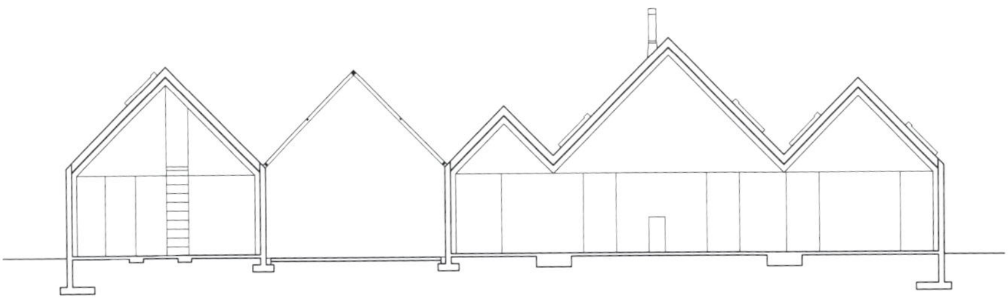

aa

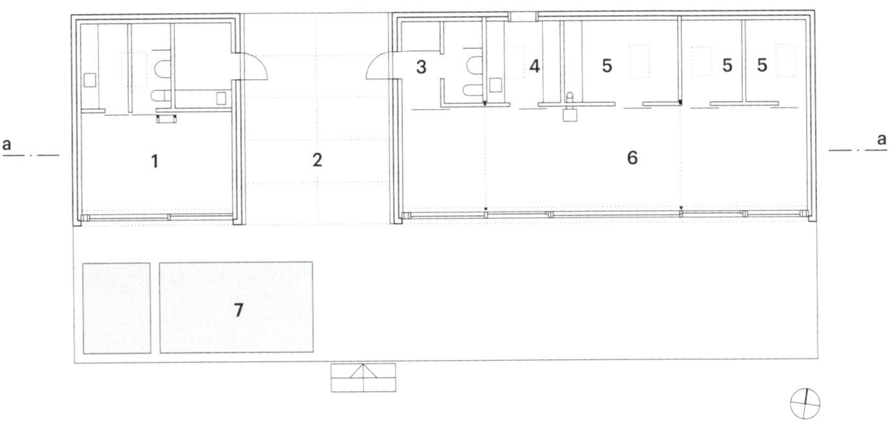

Erdgeschoss /
Ground floor

Ruinen in den Midlands

Ruins in the Midlands

Seit dem 13. Jahrhundert erfuhr Astley Castle in der englischen Grafschaft Warwickshire zahlreiche bauliche Veränderungen, bis ein Brand 1978 das Schloss weitgehend zerstörte. Mehrere Versuche des Wiederaufbaus scheiterten, sodass die Ruinen weiter verfielen – bis der historische Bau im Auftrag des Landmark Trust in ein Ferienhaus für acht Gäste umgewandelt wurde.
Die dafür verantwortlichen Architekten aus London haben im Zuge der Restaurierung die historischen Mauern durch Betonbalken verbunden, um sie zu stabilisieren, von oben schützt sie ein neu errichtetes Dach. Neues Mauerwerk schließt die Lücken in den Wänden, lässt aber gleichzeitig den Eindruck des Verfallenen, Unvollendeten bestehen. Holzbalkendecken, Holzfußböden und Fensterrahmen aus hellem Holz kontrastieren zu den roten Ziegelwänden. Die Räume aus dem 15. und 17. Jahrhundert sind heute offene Höfe, statt der früheren Deckengemälde sind nun die Wolken am Himmel zu sehen. Im unteren Geschoss liegen die Schlafräume, im ersten Stock der große Wohn- und Essbereich. Er öffnet sich mit großzügigen Verglasungen zu den Höfen sowie zur Umgebung und bindet die Ferienunterkunft so in die umliegende historische Kulturlandschaft ein.

Since the 13th century, Astley Castle, located in the English County of Warwickshire, went through numerous architectural changes and was practically destroyed by a fire in 1978. Several reconstruction attempts failed and the ruins continued to deteriorate until the Landmark Trust commissioned the conversion of the historical building to a holiday home accommodating eight persons. In the course of the restoration, the responsible London-based architects connected the historical walls with concrete beams in order to stabilise them, and fitted a new roof offering protection from above. Gaps in the walls are closed with new masonry, while at the same time leaving an impression of dilapidation and incompleteness. Wooden beam ceilings, wooden flooring and window frames made of light-coloured wood provide a contrast to the red brick walls. Rooms dating back to the 15th and 17th centuries are open courtyards today, with the clouds in the sky taking the place of former ceiling frescoes. Bedrooms can be found on the ground floor, while a large living and dining area is situated on the first floor. This opens up towards the courtyards and the exterior through generous glazing fronts, thereby integrating the holiday accommodation in the surrounding cultural landscape.

Architekten: Witherford Watson Mann Architects
Bauherr: The Landmark Trust
Tragwerksplaner: Price & Myers
Kostenplaner: Jackson Coles
Machbarkeitsstudie: Building Design Partnership
Material: Ziegel, Betonfertigteile, Holz, Klarglas
Region/Land: Warwickshire, England, Großbritanien
Funktion: Ferienhaus
Nutzung: permanent

Architects: Witherford Watson Mann Architects
Client: The Landmark Trust
Strucural engineering: Price & Myers
Quantity surveyor: Jackson Coles
Outline services design: Building Design Partnership
Material: Brick, precast concrete, laminated timber, low iron glass
Region/Country: Warwickshire, England, Great Britain
Function: Holiday home
Utilisation: Permanent

ASTLEY CASTLE, NUNEATON (GB)

Grundrisse / Schnitt
Maßstab 1:400

1 Hof
2 Halle
3 Schlafzimmer
4 Luftraum
5 Küche
6 Essbereich
7 Wohnraum

Floor plans / Section
Scale 1:400

1 Courtyard
2 Hall
3 Bedroom
4 Void over court
5 Kitchen
6 Dining area
7 Living area

aa

Erdgeschoss /
Ground floor

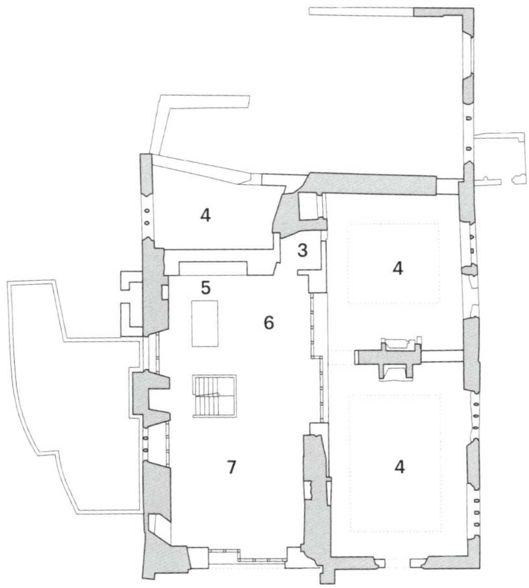

Obergeschoss /
First floor

Seetanghaus im Kattegat

Seaweed house in the Kattegat

Biobasierte Baustoffe finden seit einiger Zeit wieder vermehrt Verwendung – neben Holz sind das etwa Stampflehm, Schilf, Reet und nachwachsende Dämmstoffe. Das dänische Büro Tegnestuen Vandkunsten fügt der Palette mit dem auf der dänischen Insel Laesø im nördlichen Kattegat errichteten Ferienhaus als weiteren Werkstoff Seetang hinzu. Das Material wurde für den lang gestreckten Bau als Dachdeckung in gestrickte Schafwollnetze gestopft und diese mit Seilen außen auf der Holzlattung des Dachs befestigt. Für die Fassaden sind die Seetangnetze, die sich durch die Witterung mit der Zeit silbergrau verfärben, in vorgefertigte Holzrahmenpaneele integriert. In Dach und Wänden findet loser Seetang als Wärmedämmung Verwendung.
Und auch im Inneren kommt das Material zum Einsatz und zwar in zwei Lagen Textilien verpackt als Dachverkleidung. Diese lässt die Dachuntersicht wie gepolstert wirken und bildet eine farblich harmonische Ergänzung zum Holz von Böden und Wänden.
Dank Holzbauweise und dem Seetang als nachwachsendem Material ist der CO_2-Fußabdruck des Gebäudes minimal. Die Gebäudetechnik mit kontrollierter Be- und Entlüftung mit Wärmerückgewinnung und Luft-Wasser-Wärmepumpe unterstützt die nachhaltige Bauweise zusätzlich.

Architekten: Tegnestuen Vandkunsten
Bauherr: Realdania Byg
Tragwerksplanung: Moe
Material: Seegras, Lärche, Nadelholz
Region / Land: Laesø, Dänemark
Funktion: Ferienhaus
Nutzung: permanent

In addition to timber, biologically based building materials have enjoyed a revival for some time now. These include packed loam, reed, thatching and renewable insulation materials. The holiday home built by the Danish firm Tegnestuen Vandkunsten on the Danish island of Laesø in the northern Kattegat has added another material to this list: seaweed. This was stuffed into nets knitted out of sheep's wool and these bolsters of roofing material were fixed to wooden battens on the outside of the roof of the long building.
The seaweed nets, which turn silver-grey due to weathering in the course of time, are also integrated in the prefabricated timber frame panels of the facades. The material is packed loosely to provide thermal insulation in the roof and wall structures.
But that's not all: seaweed is also used as internal roof cladding, packed between two textile layers. This makes the underside of the roof look padded, in perfect harmony with the colours of the wooden floors and walls.
The CO_2 footprint of the building is minimal thanks to the timber frame construction and the renewable material seaweed. Sustainability of the design is further enhanced by building technology, such as an efficient ventilation system with heat recovery and an air-to-water heat pump.

Architects: Tegnestuen Vandkunsten
Client: Realdania Byg
Structural engineering: Moe
Material: Eelgrass, larch, softwood
Region / Country: Laesø, Denmark
Function: Holiday home
Utilisation: Permanent

Grundrisse / Schnitte
Maßstab 1:250

Floor plans / Sections
Scale 1:250

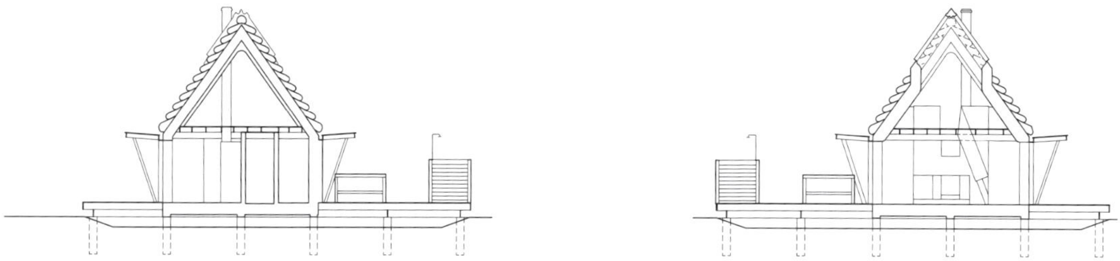

aa

bb

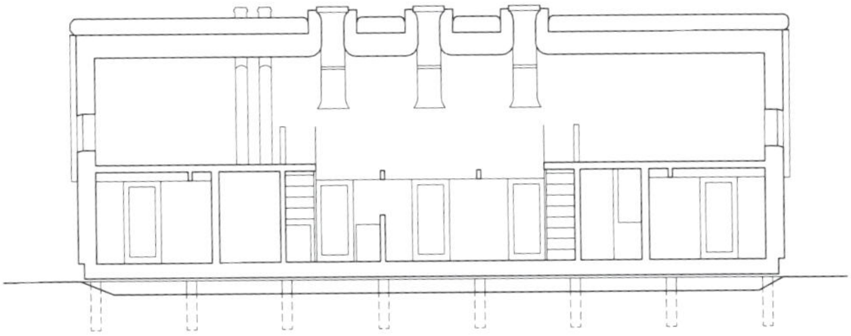

cc

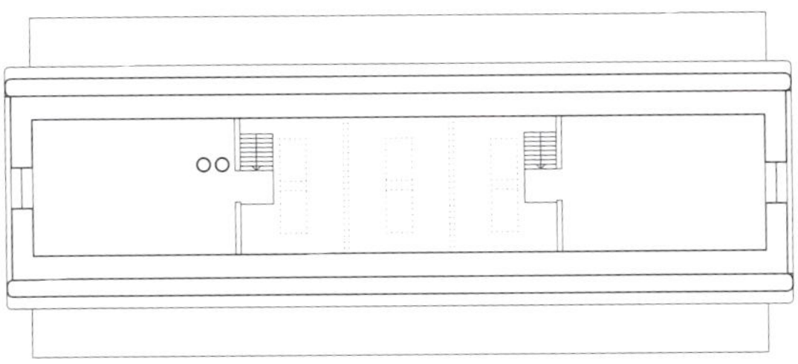

Obergeschoss /
First floor

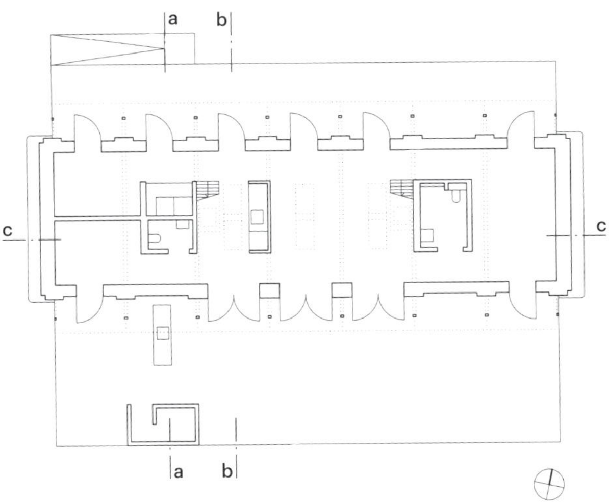

Erdgeschoss /
Ground floor

Holzhaus in der Dünenlandschaft der Pazifikküste

Timber house in dune landscape along Pacific coast

Am Sandstrand von Morillos Beach in Chile erhebt sich die flache Struktur aus der kargen Dünenlandschaft. Das Ferienhaus für bis zu sechs Personen wurde mit sparsamen Mitteln und einem klaren Raumkonzept umgesetzt. Seine äußere Form ist ein Quader, dessen Seiten rundum 72 gebäudehohe Holztüren bilden. Mit ihnen lässt sich das Gebäude wahlweise komplett nach außen zum Meer hin öffnen oder aber schrittweise von der Umgebung abschotten. Der Grundriss der Wohnräume ist dem Quadrat als Kreuz eingeschrieben, an den Ecken ist jeweils ein Patio platziert. Zu diesen öffnen sich die drei privaten Flügel mit Schlafzimmer und Bad sowie der gemeinschaftliche Wohnbereich. Er nimmt das Zentrum des Hauses ein und erhält Tageslicht von oben. Für die Konstruktion verwendete der Architekt ausschließlich Kiefernholz aus dem waldreichen Süden Chiles. Das Tragwerk besticht durch seine filigrane Ästhetik und kommt ohne verbindende Metallteile aus – alle Verbindungen sind geleimt.

A flat structure rises out of the sparse dune landscape on Chile's sandy Morillos Beach. The clear spatial concept of the holiday home for up to six persons was realised economically. The square-shaped exterior is composed of 72 doors that are as high as the building itself. This makes it possible to either open up the house fully towards the sea or shield it off from the surroundings to various degrees. The layout of the living spaces within is cruciform, with a patio placed in each corner. Three private wings containing bedrooms and bathrooms, as well as the common living area open up towards these patios. With daylight illumination from above, the common area constitutes the heart of the house. The architect used only pine, sourced from the extensively forested south of Chile, for the construction. All connections of the filigree supporting structure are glued, with no metal parts at all.

Architekten: Cristián Izquierdo Architect
Bauherr: privat
Tragwerksplanung: Osvaldo Peñaloza
Material: Holz (Kiefer)
Region/Land: Region Coquimbo, Chile
Funktion: Ferienhaus, zu mieten
Nutzung: temporär

Architects: Cristián Izquierdo Architect
Client: Private
Structural engineering: Osvaldo Peñaloza
Material: Pine wood
Region/Country: Coquimbo Region, Chile
Function: Holiday/rental home
Utilisation: Temporary

Grundriss / Schnitte
Maßstab 1:400

1 Patio
2 Schlafzimmer
3 Bad
4 Wohn- / Essbereich
5 Küche

Floor plan / Sections
Scale 1:400

1 Patio
2 Bedroom
3 Bathroom
4 Living / Dining
5 Kitchen

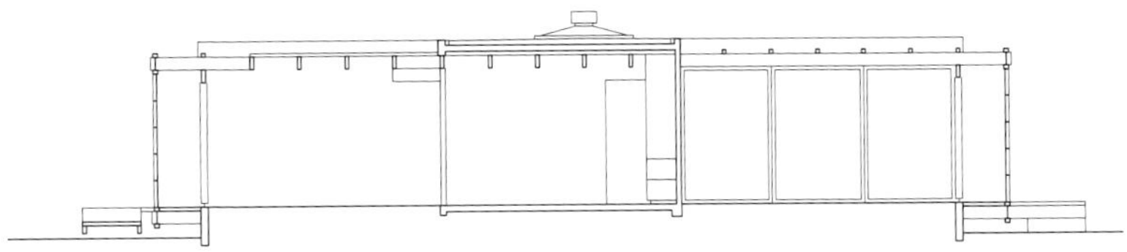

aa

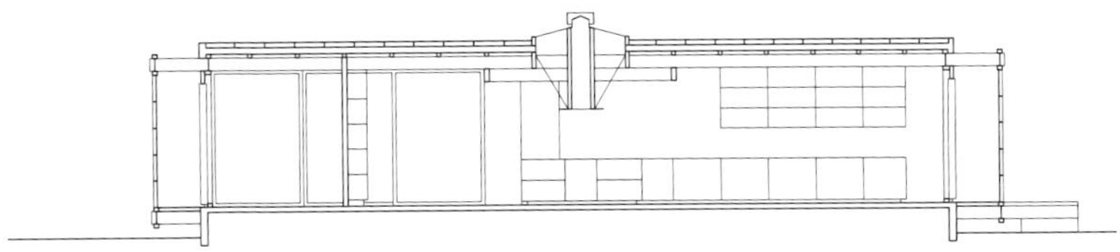

bb

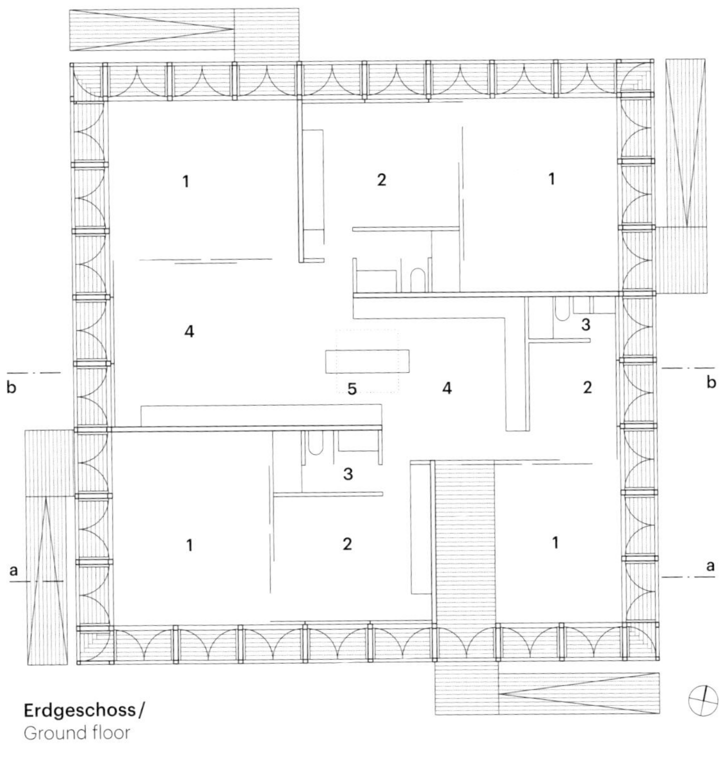

Erdgeschoss/
Ground floor

Stallhaus in der Surselva

Stable house in the Surselva region

Erst auf den zweiten Blick wird deutlich, dass dieses Haus in der Bündner Alpenlandschaft kein typischer landwirtschaftlicher Nutzbau ist. In der alten, original belassenen Hülle steht nach dem Haus-im-Haus-Prinzip eine neue Holzkonstruktion, mit der die Architekten den alten Stall samt Heulager in ein Ferienhaus verwandelt haben. Dazu wurde der Bestand weitgehend entkernt, die Deckenbalken und einige Querwände blieben jedoch erhalten. Auf diese Weise entsteht im Inneren ein deutlicher Kontrast zwischen dem neu hinzugefügten hellen Fichtenholz und den verwitterten alten Teilen. Der neue Fußboden, ein fast schwarzer pigmentierter Zementestrich, verbindet alle Räume. Die im Strickbau errichteten ursprünglichen Stallwände aus unregelmäßigen Balken hüllen die neue Fassade ein. Sie bilden eine zweite Schicht, die als Sonnenschutz dient, in den Bädern und Schlafbereichen für Privatsphäre sorgt und gleichzeitig wechselnde Ausblicke in die Landschaft rahmt. Von außen betrachtet fügt sich das Stallhaus dank dem behutsamen Umgang mit dem historischen Bestand harmonisch in die gewachsene Struktur des Alpendorfs ein.

Architekten: Morger Partner Architekten/ Morger + Dettli Architekten
Bauherr: privat
Bauingenieur: Conzett Bronzini Gartmann
Haustechnik: Waldhauser + Hermann
Material: Fichtenholz, Beton
Region/Land: Graubünden, Schweiz
Funktion: Ferienhaus
Nutzung: temporär

You need to look twice to realise that this house in the midst of the Bündner Alps is not actually an agriculturally used building. Based on the house-within-a-house principle, the architects transformed the old stable and hayloft into a holiday home by placing a new timber construction inside the untouched original exterior shell. The building was extensively gutted, while the ceiling beams and some cross walls were retained. A clear contrast between old weathered parts and newly added light spruce elements is created in the interior in this way. All spaces are connected by an almost black pigmented cement screed constituting the new flooring. The new facade is encased with the irregular logs used to construct the original stable walls. They form a second layer, which provides solar protection, creates privacy in the bathrooms and bedrooms, while at the same time framing changing views of the landscape. The stable house fits harmoniously into the established structure of the alpine village, thanks to the sensitivity with which this historical building has been converted.

Architects: Morger Partner Architekten/ Morger + Dettli Architekten
Client: Private
Structural engineering: Conzett Bronzini Gartmann
Building services: Waldhauser + Hermann
Material: Concrete, spruce
Region/Country: Graubunden, Switzerland
Function: Holiday home
Utilisation: Temporary

Grundrisse / Schnitt
Maßstab 1:400

1 Eingang
2 Schlafen
3 Waschraum
4 Haustechnik
5 Stube
6 Speisekammer

Floor plans / Section
Scale 1:400

1 Entrance
2 Bedroom
3 Laundry room
4 Services
5 Living / Dining
6 Pantry

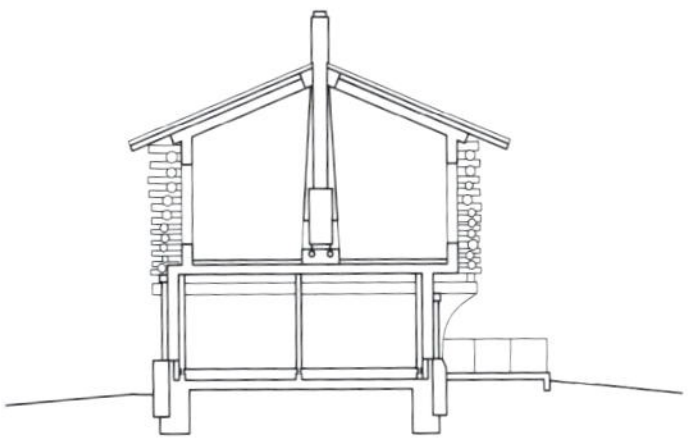

aa

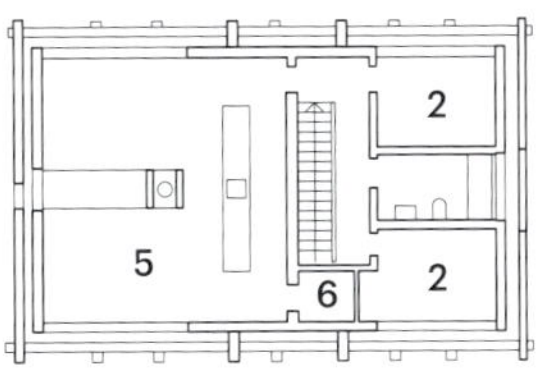

Obergeschoss /
First floor

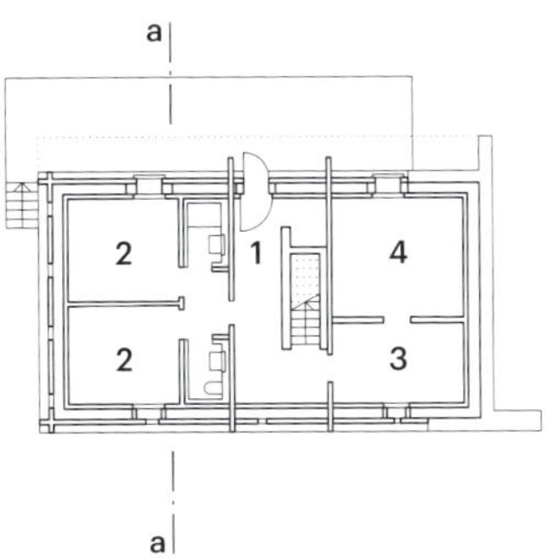

Erdgeschoss /
Ground floor

Dachlandschaft auf Seeland

Roof landscape on Zealand

Die strengen Bauvorschriften erlaubten für den Bungalow aus den 1960er-Jahren auf einem Grundstück mit altem Baumbestand weder eine Erweiterung der Grundfläche noch ein Obergeschoss. Um den zusätzlichen Flächenbedarf der Familie mit drei Kindern zu decken, entwickelten die Architekten eine recht individuelle Idee: Mithilfe verschieden großer Dachaufbauten schufen sie 35 zusätzliche Quadratmeter Wohnfläche – einen Arbeitsbereich über dem Elternschlafzimmer, Schlafemporen für die Kinderzimmer im Erdgeschoss und ein drittes Kinderzimmer auf dem Dach. Horizontale Oberlichter in den skulpturalen Aufbauten holen den Himmel und viel Licht in die Räume.
Nach außen hin gibt sich die anthrazitfarbene Ziegelfassade mit nur wenigen kleinen Öffnungen eher verschlossen. Doch nach innen hin öffnet sich das u-förmige Haus fast vollständig verglast zu einem als Terrasse genutzten Hof. Zwei weitere trichterförmige Volumen über Küche und Wohnbereich bringen zusätzlich Licht in die Räume. Auf diese Weise verbindet sich das Gebäude in alle Richtungen mit den umstehenden Bäumen und dem wechselnden Licht, das durch die Äste fällt, und macht die Natur erlebbar.

Architekten: Leth & Gori
Bauherr: privat
Tragwerksplanung: Jørgen Nielsen Rådgivende Ingeniører
Material: Ziegel, Holz, Zink, Bitumen
Region / Land: Fredensborg, Dänemark
Funktion: Wohnhaus
Nutzung: permanent

Strict building regulations permitted neither an extension of the footprint of the 1960s bungalow, located on a plot with old trees on it, nor the addition of an upper storey. To meet the need for more space of the family with three children, the architects came up with a rather individual idea: they used roof structures of various sizes to create an additional 35 square metres of living space – a study above the master bedroom, sleeping lofts for the rooms of the children on the ground floor and a third child's room under the roof. Horizontal skylights in the sculptural structures allow a view of the sky and plenty of light to enter the rooms.
A closed impression is created to the outside, with only a few small openings in the anthracite-coloured brick facade. Almost fully glazed towards the inside however, the U-shaped house opens up to a courtyard used as a terrace. Additional light is admitted to the kitchen and living area by means of two further funnel-shaped volumes. This opens up the building in all directions and creates a connection to the nearby trees and the changing light falling through their branches, bringing nature inside the house.

Architects: Leth & Gori
Client: Private
Structural engineering: Jørgen Nielsen Rådgivende Ingeniører
Material: Brick, wood, zinc, asphalt roofing
Region / Country: Fredensborg, Denmark
Function: Residence
Utilisation: Permanent

Grundriss / Schnitte
Maßstab 1:250

1 Eingang
2 Diele
3 Küche
4 Ess-/Wohnbereich
5 Hauswirtschaftsraum
6 Kinderzimmer
7 Ankleide
8 Schlafzimmer

Floor plan / Sections
Scale 1:250

1 Entrance
2 Entrance hall
3 Kitchen
4 Dining/Living room
5 Utility room
6 Child's bedroom
7 Dressing room
8 Bedroom

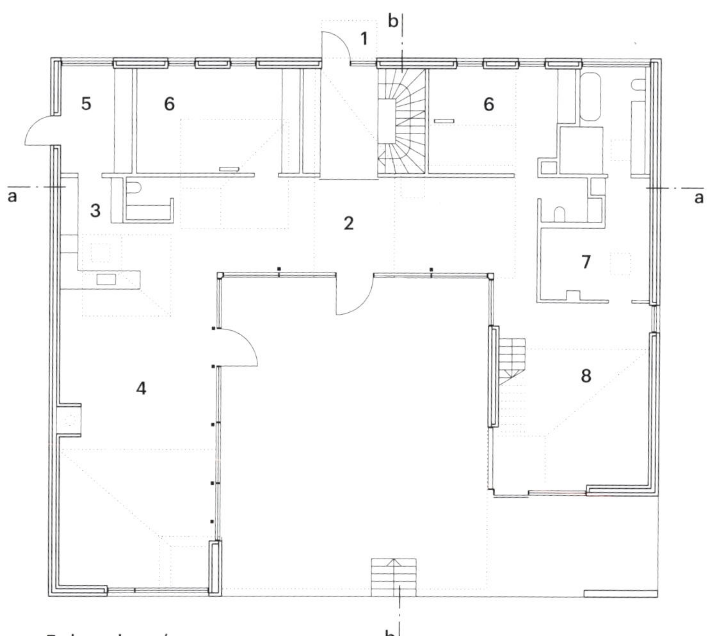

Erdgeschoss /
Ground floor

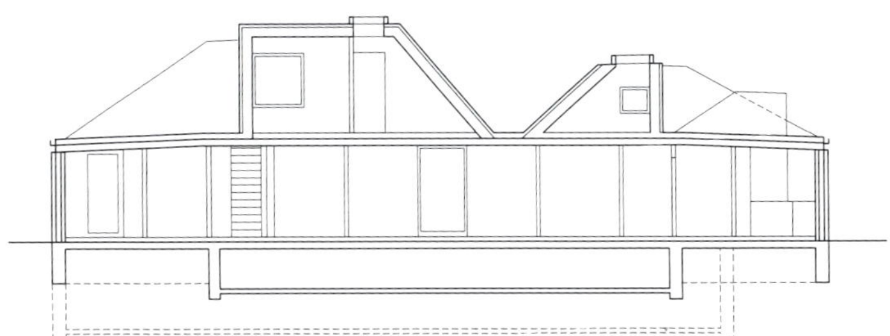

aa

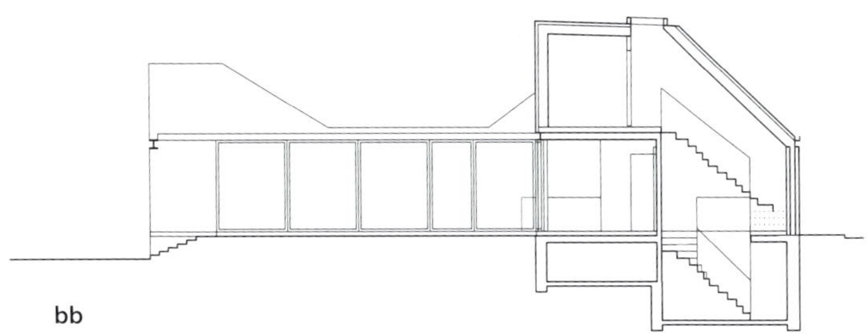

bb

Neue Bau-tradition im Karst

New building tradition in the Karst region

Einst war der Karst im Hinterland der Triester Bucht von dichten Eichenwäldern bewachsen. Doch die Venezianer holzten die Baumbestände ab, zurück blieb eine zerklüftete Felslandschaft. Die traditionellen Häuser der Region sind aus Stein gebaut, sehr introvertiert und kommen fast ohne Fenster aus. Die Architekten griffen mit ihrem Entwurf auf diese typische Bauweise zurück, interpretierten sie jedoch für das Einfamilienhaus auf zeitgenössische Art. Um dem Baukörper aus Stahlbeton und Ziegel einen monolithischen Charakter zu verleihen, erhielt die Fassade eine äußere Schicht aus Stein und Beton. Dafür wurde in eine Schalung vor dem Ziegel Kalkstein eingelegt und mit Mörtel vergossen. Der überschüssige Mörtel in den Fugen wurde dann nur grob entfernt und erzeugt auf diese Weise eine lebendige Wirkung. Das abgetreppte Dach ohne Überstände besteht aus Stahlbeton und weckt Assoziationen an eine Steinplatte.
Im Inneren gliedert eine Haus-im-Haus-Struktur aus Holz die Räume. Wenige, für die Region ungewöhnlich große Fenster rahmen die Ausblicke in die Umgebung und weisen den archetypischen Satteldachbau als modernes Wohnhaus aus.

The Karst region in the hinterland of the Gulf of Trieste used to be covered by dense oak forests, until they were cut down by the Venetians, leaving a craggy landscape dominated by rocks. Houses in the region are traditionally built of stone and with hardly any windows, they tend to be very introverted. The architects based the design of the their single-family home on a contemporary interpretation of this vernacular architecture. The reinforced concrete and brick structure was given a monolithic character by adding an outer layer of stone and concrete to the facade. To this end, formwork was erected in front of the brick masonry and filled with limestone rocks and mortar. Excess mortar in the joints was removed only roughly, producing a lively effect. The stepped roof without any overhang consists of reinforced concrete and calls to mind a stone plate.
A wooden house-within-a-house structure organises the rooms inside. Few but exceptionally large windows for the region frame views of the surrounding nature, unambiguously identifying the archetypical gable roof construction as a modern residential house.

Architekten: dekleva gregorič architects
Bauherr: Borut Pertot
Tragwerksplanung: Luka Pavlovčič
Material: Beton, Ziegel, Sperrholz
Region/Land: Karst, Slowenien
Funktion: Wohnhaus
Nutzung: permanent

Architects: dekleva gregorič architects
Client: Borut Pertot
Structural engineering: Luka Pavlovčič
Material: Concrete, brick, massive solid plywood
Region/Country: Karst, Slovenia
Function: Residence
Utilisation: Permanent

Grundrisse / Schnitte
Maßstab 1:250

1 Eingang
2 Kamin
3 Bad
4 Küche / Esszimmer
5 Einbauschrank
6 Kinderschlafzimmer
7 Spielbrücke
8 Luftraum
9 Schlafzimmer

Floor plans / Sections
Scale 1:250

1 Entrance
2 Chimney
3 Bathroom
4 Kitchen / Dining
5 Built-in closet
6 Children's bedroom
7 Bridge as play space
8 Void
9 Bedroom

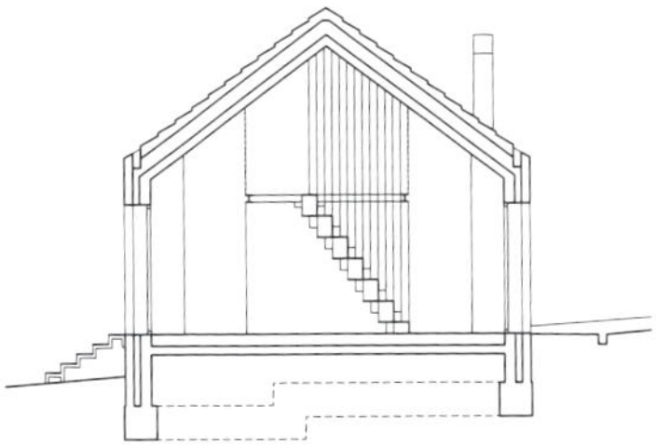

aa

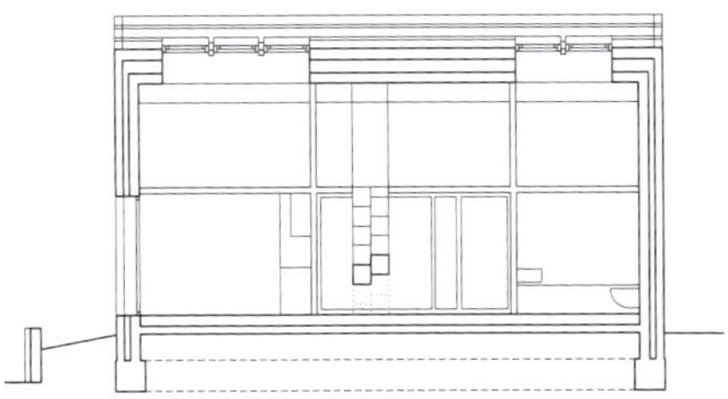

bb

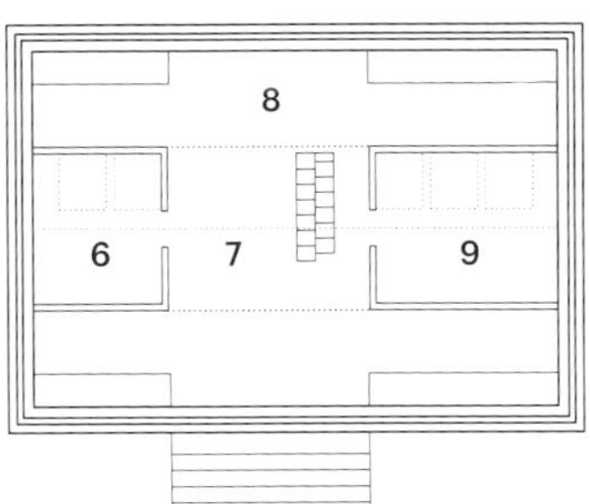

Obergeschoss /
First floor

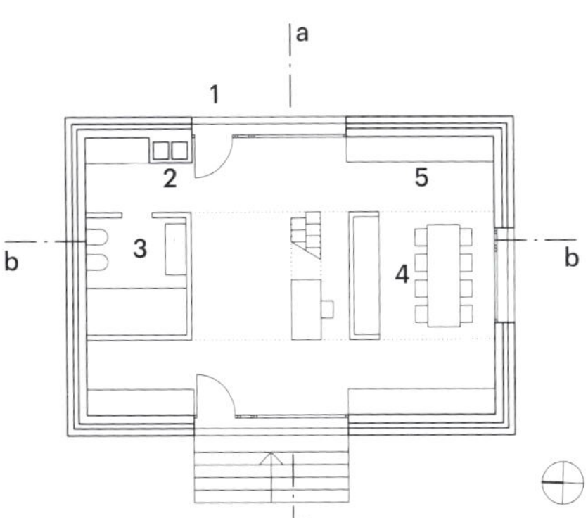

Erdgeschoss /
Ground floor

Grüne Mitte in der Extremadura

Green focus in the Extremadura province

Um den Verfall des kleinen Dorfs Cilleros im Westen von Spanien aufzuhalten, sind dort Häuser zu sehr günstigen Preisen erhältlich – mit der Auflage, dass sie restauriert werden müssen. Für den verfallenen, schmalen Bau, mit dessen Umbau Arquitectura-G beauftragt wurde, stand nur ein kleines Budget zur Verfügung. Daher entschieden sich die Architekten, lediglich die Steinfassaden und die Haustrennwände aus Lehm stehen zu lassen und das Innere zu entkernen. In der neu errichteten Konstruktion ordnen sich drei Ebenen komplett verglast um einen Innenhof, der viel Licht und Luft in die Räume bringt. Die minimalistische Struktur aus weißen Stahlträgern und weiß getünchten Wänden in Kombination mit keramischen Deckenelementen in Rot erzeugt einen grafischen Effekt.
Den Mittelpunkt des Neubaus bildet die im Innenhof gepflanzte Birke. Sie sorgt im heißen Sommer für natürlichen Sonnenschutz, lässt aber die tiefer stehende Wintersonne ins Haus fallen. Als lebendiges, natürliches Element macht sie den Wechsel der Tages- und Jahreszeiten im Haus erlebbar und verwandelt Küche und Wohnbereich, die zwischen dem Innenhof und dem Garten hinter dem Haus liegen, in grüne Zimmer.

Architekten: Arquitectura-G
Bauherr: privat
Tragwerksplanung: Toni Casas/Upuntsis
Material: Steinfassade, Lehmwände (Bestand), Keramikfliesen, Metall, Gewebe (Revitalisierung)
Region/Land: Cáceres, Extremadura, Spanien
Funktion: Wohnhaus
Nutzung: temporär

In an attempt to check the decline of the small village of Cilleros in western Spain, houses are offered at very good prices – with the condition that they must be renovated. Only a small budget was available for the conversion of the derelict, narrow building for which Arquitectura-G was commissioned. The architects therefore decided to simply leave the stone facades and inner dividing walls made of loam unchanged and gut the building. In the new construction, three fully glazed levels surround an inner courtyard, admitting plenty of light and air to the rooms. A graphic effect is achieved by the minimalistic structure made of white steel girders and white painted walls in combination with red ceramic ceiling elements. The birch tree planted in the courtyard forms the focus of the new construction. It provides natural protection from the sun in the hot summers, and allows the lower winter sun to penetrate the space with natural light. As a living, natural element, the tree communicates the different times of the day and the seasons of the year to the occupants of the house, while also turning the kitchen and living areas located between the courtyard and the garden into green rooms.

Architects: Arquitectura-G
Client: Private
Structural engineering: Toni Casas/Upuntsis
Material: Stone facade, mud walls (existing), ceramic tiles, metal, mesh (refurbishment)
Region/Country: Cáceres, Extremadura, Spain
Function: Residence
Utilisation: Temporary

Grundrisse / Schnitt
Maßstab 1:250

1 Straßeneingang
2 offene Halle
3 Garteneingang
4 Küche
5 Schlafzimmer
6 Wohnzimmer

Floor plans / Section
Scale 1:250

1 Street entrance
2 Open hall
3 Garden entrance
4 Kitchen
5 Bedroom
6 Living room

CASA LUZ, CILLEROS (ES)

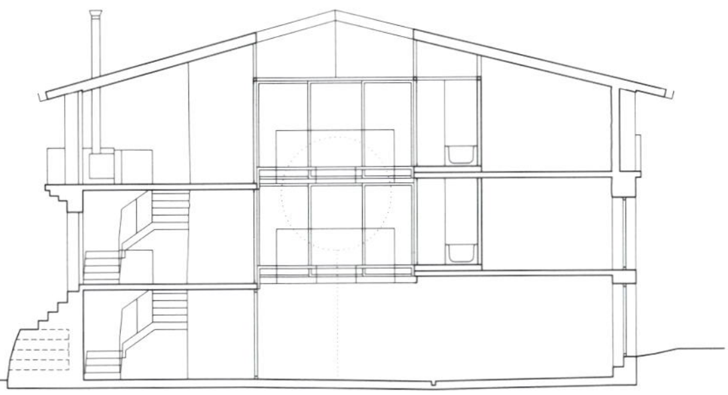

aa

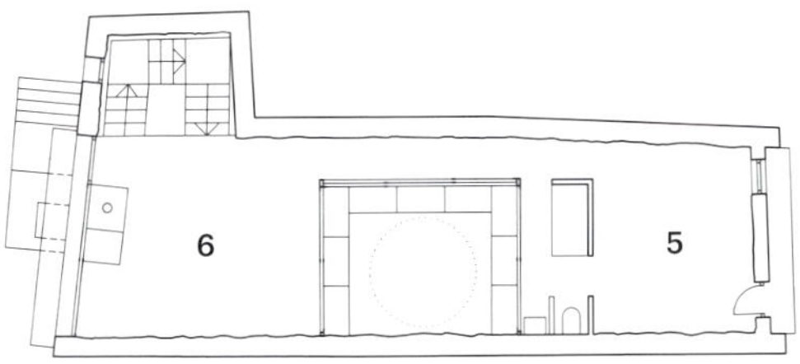

2. Obergeschoss/
Second floor

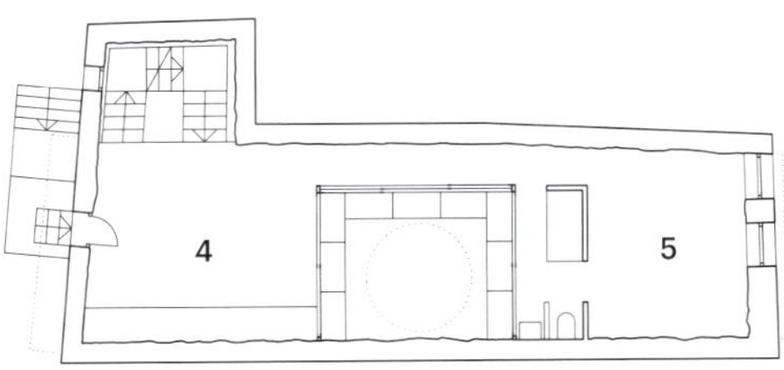

1. Obergeschoss/
First floor

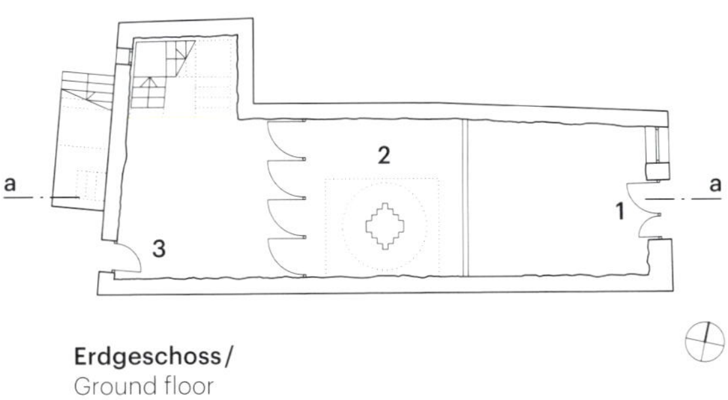

Erdgeschoss/
Ground floor

Blockhaus im norwegischen Kiefernwald

Log cabin in Norwegian pine forest

Am Ufer des Femundsees, in Norwegens kältester Region südlich des Polarkreises, liegt dieses ungewöhnliche Ferienhaus. Die beiden langen Satteldachbaukörper überkreuzen sich. Sie bestehen aus zwei alten, einfachen Blockhäusern, die um einen polygonalen Neubau ergänzt wurden. Da das Ensemble auf 50 Zentimeter hohen Punktfundamenten ruht, schwebt es gleichsam über der umliegenden Vegetation und setzt sich von ihr ab. Ein umlaufendes Holzdeck verknüpft Alt und Neu. Beide Teile sind in traditioneller Blockbauweise errichtet – für die Erweiterung wurde lokale Kiefer verwendet. Damit sie den Farbton des verwitterten Bestands aufnehmen, sind die neuen Fassaden mit Eisensulfat gebeizt. Auf dem Dach wechseln sich Stahlwellblech und Polycarbonatplatten ab. Das transluzente Material findet auch über den Fensteröffnungen Verwendung und wirkt der Verschattung durch den großen Dachüberstand entgegen. Auch der zentrale Eingangshof und die Terrassen sind komplett damit überdeckt und erhalten auf diese Weise Tageslicht.
Die alten Hütten beherbergen einen Lagerraum und ein Gästezimmer, der Neubau nimmt weitere Wohnfunktionen auf. Große Fenster rahmen den Ausblick über den See und in die weite skandinavische Landschaft.

Located on the shores of Lake Femunden, this unusual holiday home is situated in the coldest region of Norway to the south of the polar circle. The two long intersecting gable roof structures are composed of a pair of simple old log cabins that were supplemented by a new polygonal construction. Resting on 50-centimetres-high spot footings, the raised ensemble appears to float above the surrounding vegetation. Old and new are linked by a wooden deck running around the cruciform shape. Both parts are constructed as traditional log structures, with local pine used for the extension. The new facades were stained with iron sulphate to make them match the older weathered fabric. An alternation of corrugated iron and polycarbonate panels covers the roof. Integration of the translucent material above the window openings counteracts the shading effect of a generous roof overhang. Polycarbonate is also used to cover the central entrance deck and terraces, allowing daylight illumination of these areas.
The old cabins contain storage space and a guest room, while the new structure accommodates further residential functions. Large windows frame views across the lake and of the rambling Scandinavian landscape.

Architekten: Aslak Haanshuus Arkitekter
Bauherr: privat
Tragwerksplaner: Martin Røsand
Material: (heimisches) Kiefernholz, Stahlwellblech, Polycarbonatplatten, Verglasung in Holz-Aluminiumrahmen
Region / Land: Hedmark, Norwegen
Funktion: Ferienhaus
Nutzung: permanent

Architects: Aslak Haanshuus Arkitekter
Client: Private
Structural engineering: Martin Røsand
Material: Local timber, corrugated steel sheets, Velfac windows
Region / Country: Hedmark, Norway
Function: Holiday home
Utilisation: Permanent

Grundriss
Maßstab 1:250

1 Eingangsbereich
2 Diele
3 Schlafraum
4 Küche
5 Wohn-/Essbereich
6 Bad
7 Sauna
8 Technik
9 Blockhaus (Bestand)/Hauswirtschaftsraum
10 Blockhaus (Bestand)/Gästezimmer
11 Terrasse

Floor plan
Scale 1:250

1 Entrance deck
2 Entrance hall
3 Bedroom
4 Kitchen
5 Living/Dining
6 Bathroom
7 Sauna
8 Services
9 Log cabin (existing)/Utility room
10 Log cabin (existing)/Guest room
11 Terrace

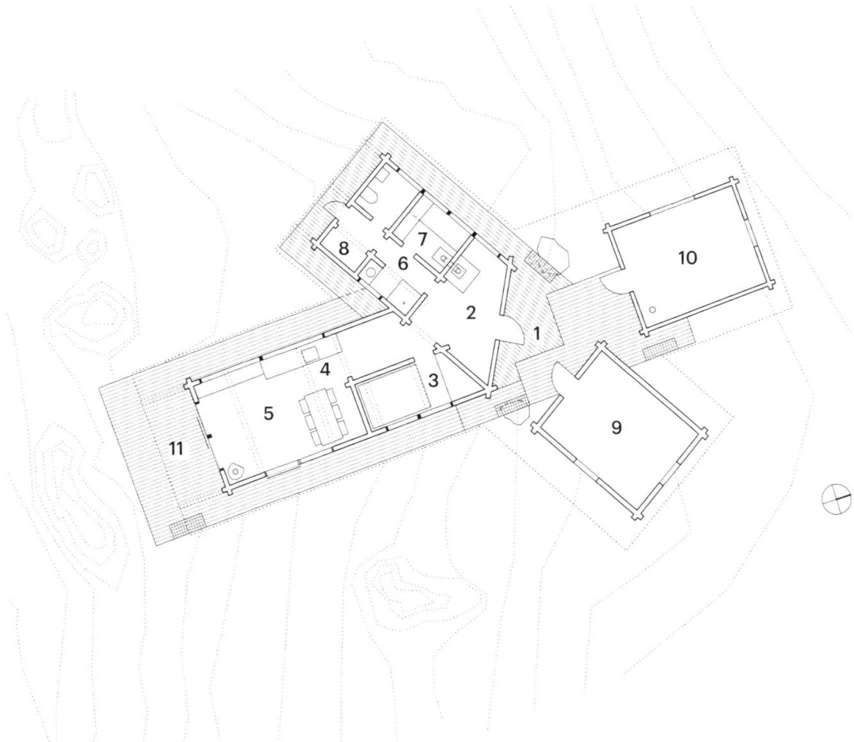

In der Vulkanlandschaft auf den Azoren

In the volcanic landscape of the Azores

Häuser aus Vulkangestein sind typisch für die Bautradition der Azoreninsel Pico. In die Ruine eines solchen Bauwerks aus dunklem Basalt platzierten die Architekten einen schlichten Sichtbetonbau. Der verfallene Bestand wurde dabei nicht verändert und das bis heute landwirtschaftlich genutzte Grundstück in seiner ursprünglichen Form erhalten, was auch für den Bauherren wichtig war. Der neue Baukörper aus einfachen geometrischen Formen ist statisch unabhängig zwischen die erhaltenen Mauern gesetzt. Die hellen, glatten Betonflächen heben sich vom dunklen Basalt ab und werden sich mit der Zeit durch die Witterung verfärben. Ziel war es, viel Licht in die Innenräume des Ferienhauses zu holen. So hält die neue Fassade Abstand von den Bestandsmauern, um Innenhöfe und Zwischenräume zu bilden. Da die Fensteröffnungen nicht immer übereinstimmen, entsteht ein reizvoller Dialog zwischen Alt und Neu sowie eine enge Verknüpfung von innen und außen. Während die Schlafräume im Erdgeschoss intimer sind, bieten sich in den Wohnräumen im Obergeschoss Ausblicke in die üppige grüne Vegetation der vulkanischen Landschaft und bis zur benachbarten Insel São Jorge.

On Pico Island in the Azores, traditional houses are made of volcanic rock. The architects placed a simple fair-faced concrete construction in the ruin of such a dark basalt building. The crumbling fabric was left unchanged and the original shape of the still agriculturally used plot of land was retained. This was an important requirement of the client. Though hugged by the preserved walls, the new volume composed of simple geometric shapes is statically independent. The smooth, light concrete surfaces contrast with the dark basalt and will weather in the course of time. The aim was to admit as much light as possible to the interior of the holiday home. Inner courtyards and interspaces are formed by gaps between the facade and the existing walls. Occasionally incoherent window openings create a charming dialogue between old and new as well as a close connection between inside and outside. While the bedrooms on the ground floor are more intimate, the living areas in the upper storey offer views of the lush green vegetation of the volcanic landscape extending all the way to the neighbouring island of São Jorge.

Architekten: SAMI-Arquitectos
Bauherr: privat
Tragwerksplaner: Ricardo Ferro Antunes, Francisco Mendonça Santos
Sanitär: Paulo Jorge Almeida Oliveira
Elektrotechnik: Hugo Mendonça
Material: Beton, Basalt, Holz
Region/Land: Azoren, Portugal
Funktion: Ferienhaus
Nutzung: temporär

Architects: SAMI-Arquitectos
Client: Private
Structural engineering: Ricardo Ferro Antunes, Francisco Mendonça Santos
Water and sanitation: Paulo Jorge Almeida Oliveira
Electrical engineering: Hugo Mendonça
Material: concrete, basalt stone, wood
Region/Country: Azores, Portugal
Function: Holiday home
Utilisation: Temporary

Grundrisse / Schnitte
Maßstab 1:250

Layout plans / Sections
Scale 1:250

1	**Schlafzimmer**	1	Bedroom
2	**Terrasse**	2	Terrace
3	**Flur**	3	Hallway
4	**Abstellkammer**	4	Closet
5	**offener Herd (Bestand)**	5	Hearth (existing)
6	**Essbereich**	6	Dining area
7	**Küche**	7	Kitchen
8	**Eingang**	8	Entrance
9	**Wohnraum**	9	Living room
10	**Balkon**	10	Balcony
11	**Zisterne (Bestand)**	11	Cistern (existing)

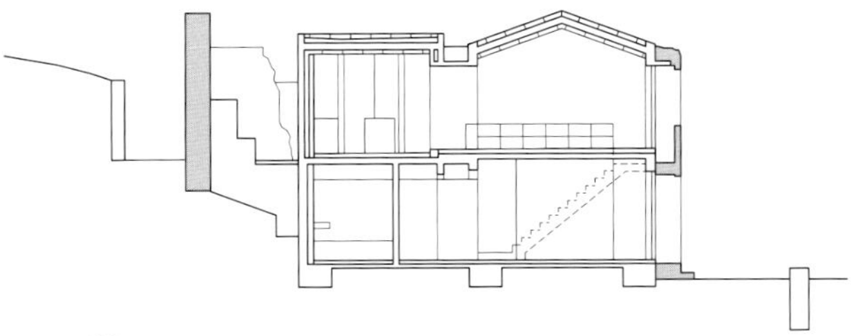

aa

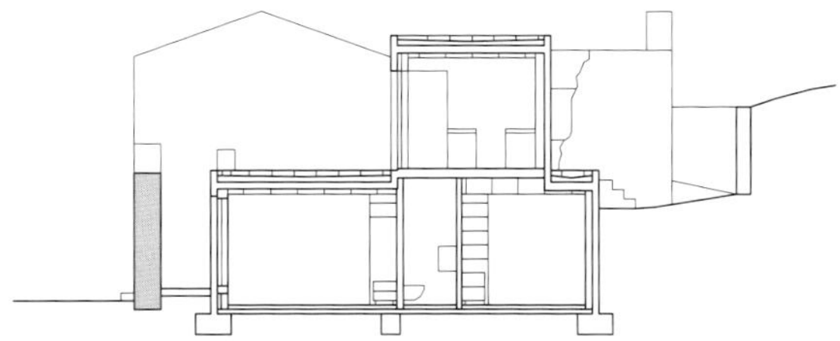

bb

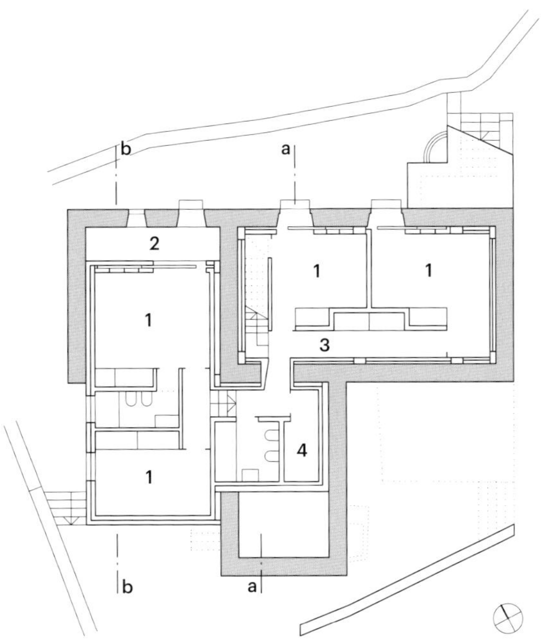

Erdgeschoss/
Ground floor

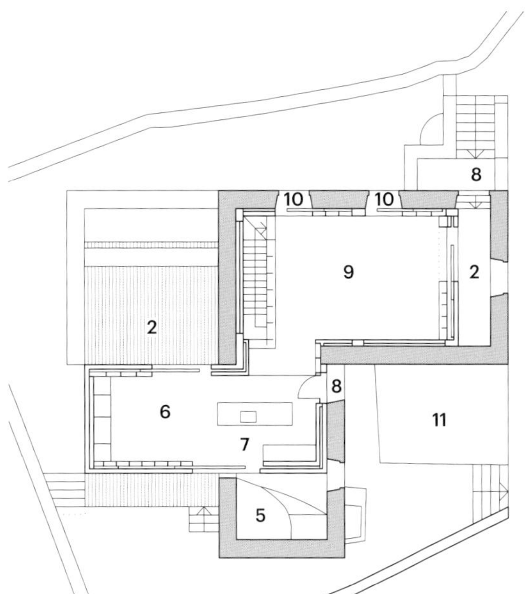

Obergeschoss/
First floor

Hochalpines Biwak in der Felslandschaft des Kanin

High alpine bivouac in the rocky landscape of the Kanin Mountains

Mitten in der zerklüfteten Felslandschaft im Kanin-Massiv an der slowenisch-italienischen Grenze balanciert dieser schimmernde polygonale Baukörper. Die schlichte Unterkunft dient als Winterbiwak, wenn die benachbarte Berghütte geschlossen hat. Extreme Wetter- und Temperaturverhältnisse sowie der schwer zugängliche Standort auf 2260 Metern Höhe waren maßgebliche Herausforderung für die Architekten. Zudem bestand der Wunsch, möglichst wenig in die natürliche Umgebung einzugreifen. Entstanden ist ein kompaktes, nur 2,40 mal 4,90 Meter großes Volumen. Es wurde im Tal als Holzkonstruktion vorfabriziert und dann per Helikopter an seinen Bestimmungsort transportiert. Dort wurde es mit Aluminiumplatten verkleidet, mittels Stahlplatten in einem Betonfundament verschraubt und zusätzlich durch sechs Stahlseile gesichert. Zum Tal hin ragt der halbe Baukörper über den Fels hinaus in der Luft. Die Schmalseite ist hier großflächig verglast und bietet atemberaubende Ausblicke, die an klaren Tagen bis zur Adria reichen. Der schlichte Innenraum ist vollständig mit Holz ausgekleidet und nimmt Schlafplätze für bis zu neun Personen auf.

Architekten: OFIS Arhitekti
Bauherr: PD Bovec
Tragwerksplanung / Generalunternehmer: CBD Contemporary Building Design
Tragwerksplanung Gründung: Milan Sorc Projecta
Material: Stahlbeton (Fundament), Aluminiumverbundplatte, Holz, Brettsperrholz, Glas
Region / Land: Kanin-Massiv, Slowenien
Funktion: Winterunterkunft
Nutzung: temporär

On the Slovenian-Italian border, this glistening polygonal structure balances right in the middle of the jagged, rocky landscape of the Kanin Mountains. The simple accommodation serves as a winter bivouac, when the neighbouring mountain hut is closed. Extreme weather and temperature conditions as well as difficult accessibility at an altitude of 2,260 metres presented a considerable challenge for the architects. The wish to interfere as little as possible in the natural environment was another factor to be taken into account. A compact volume measuring only 2.40 by 4.90 metres was created. After prefabrication of the timber construction in the valley, it was transported to the designated site by helicopter, where it was clad with aluminium panels. The structure was screwed to a concrete foundation with the help of steel plates and additionally secured by means of six steel ropes. Half of the bivouac projects beyond the rock face towards the valley unsupported. The narrow side is generously glazed, permitting breathtaking views all the way to the Adriatic Sea on clear days. The plain interior is entirely clad with wood and offers enough space to sleep for up to nine people.

Architects: OFIS Arhitekti
Client: PD Bovec
Structural engineering and principal contractor: CBD Contemporary Building Design
Structural engineering for foundation: Milan Sorc Projecta
Material: Concrete (foundation), aluminium composite panel, timber / cross-laminated timber, glass
Region/Country: Kanin Mountains, Slovenia
Function: Mountain shelter
Utilisation: Temporary

Grundriss / Schnitte
Maßstab 1:100

Floor plan / Sections
Scale 1:100

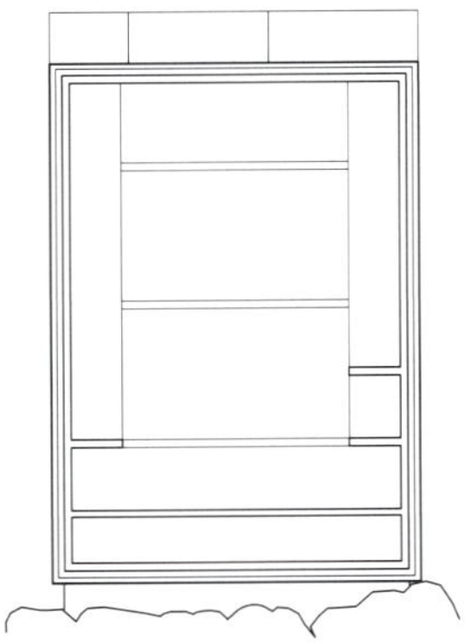

aa

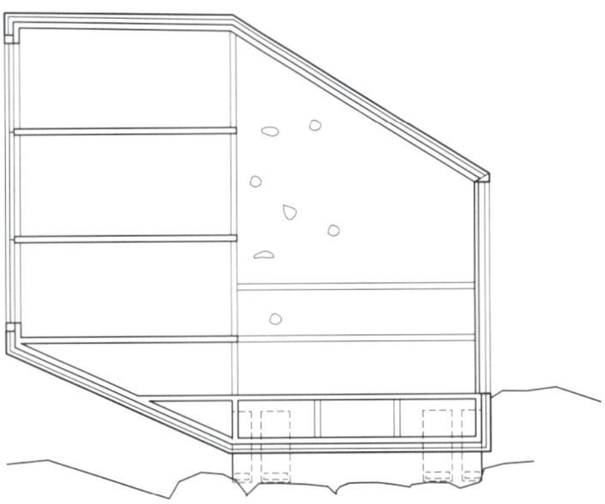

bb

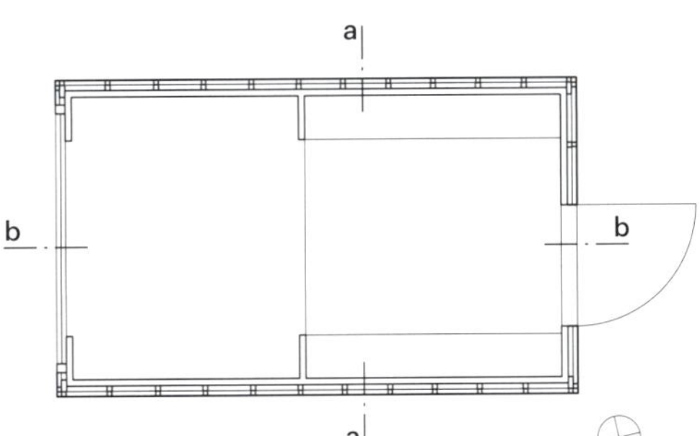

Erdgeschoss /
Ground floor

Mit der isländischen Landschaft verschmolzen

Integrated in the Icelandic landscape

Die beiden identischen Ferienhäuser sind in die schroffe arktische Landschaft im Südwesten von Island eingebettet. Der Erdaushub der Baustelle wurde als Windschutzwall für die Terrassen verwendet und schafft nahtlose Übergänge von der Dachlandschaft der Gebäude zu den Hügeln der Umgebung. Die Vegetation, die für die Grundfläche der Häuser abgetragen werden musste, wächst nun auf den Gründächern weiter und sorgt dafür, dass Architektur und Natur verschmelzen – eine zeitgenössische Interpretation traditioneller isländischer Torfhöfe.
Ein klarer Grundriss mit minimalen Erschließungsflächen charakterisiert die als Holzkonstruktion errichteten Cottages. Außen sind sie mit einer Lattung aus geflämmtem Hartholz verkleidet, die naturbelassen im Inneren an den Decken wieder auftaucht. Aus den zurückhaltend gestalteten Räumen geben großzügige Glasflächen den Blick auf die nahen Berge und den Laugarvatn-See frei. Ökologische Standards spielten beim Bau eine wichtige Rolle. In Kombination mit der geothermischen Energieversorgung ist der Betrieb der Häuser quasi emissionsfrei.

The two identical holiday cottages are embedded in the stark Arctic landscape of south-western Iceland. The earth excavated from the building site was used to form a wind barrier for the terraces, while at the same time creating a seamless transition from the roof landscape of the houses to the surrounding hills. The vegetation that had to make way for the footprints of the buildings now continues to grow on their green roofs, blending architecture with nature – a contemporary interpretation of traditional Icelandic turf houses.
The timber constructions are characterised by a clear layout with minimal circulation areas. The exterior is clad with battens of flame-finished hardwood, an untreated form of which reappears on the interior ceilings. Thanks to extensive glazing, the restrained interior permits a view of the nearby mountains and Laugarvatn Lake. Ecological standards played an important role in the construction. In combination with geothermal energy, operation of the houses is virtually emission free.

Architekten: PK Arkitektar
Bauherr: Bandalag Háskólamanna BHM, Association of Academics of Iceland
Tragwerksplaner: Verkfræðistofa Þráinn og Benedikt
Material: Holzkonstruktion auf Betonplatten, geflämmtes Hartholz
Region / Land: Brekkuskógur, Island
Funktion: Ferienhäuser
Nutzung: permanent

Architects: PK Arkitektar
Client: Bandalag Háskólamanna BHM, Association of Academics of Iceland
Structural engineering: Verkfræðistofa Þráinn og Benedikt
Material: Timber construction on a concrete slab, cladding made of hardwood strips with charred finish
Region / Country: Brekkuskógur, Iceland
Function: Holiday homes
Utilisation: Permanent

Grundriss / Schnitte
Maßstab 1:250

1 Zimmer
2 Küche
3 Wohn-/Esszimmer
4 Abstellraum
5 Müllraum
6 »Hot Pot«

Floor plan / Sections
Scale 1:250

1 Room
2 Kitchen
3 Living-/Dining
4 Storage
5 Trash room
6 Hot tub

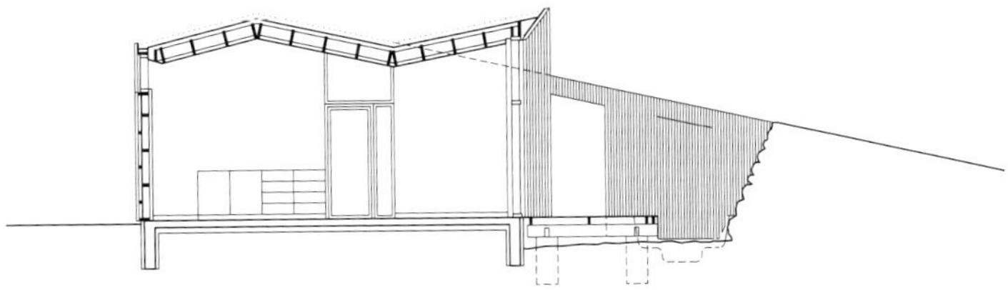

aa

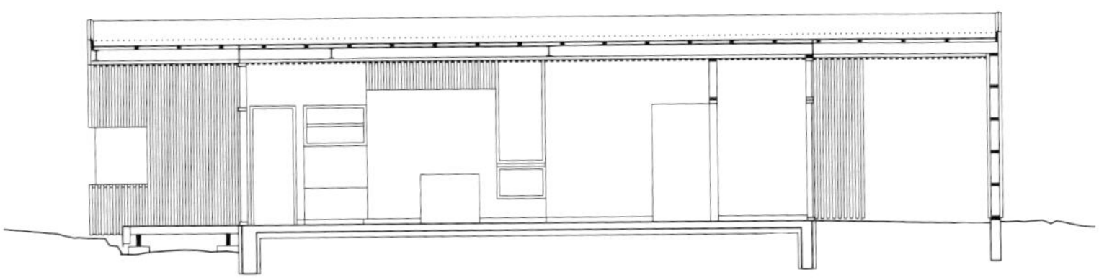

bb

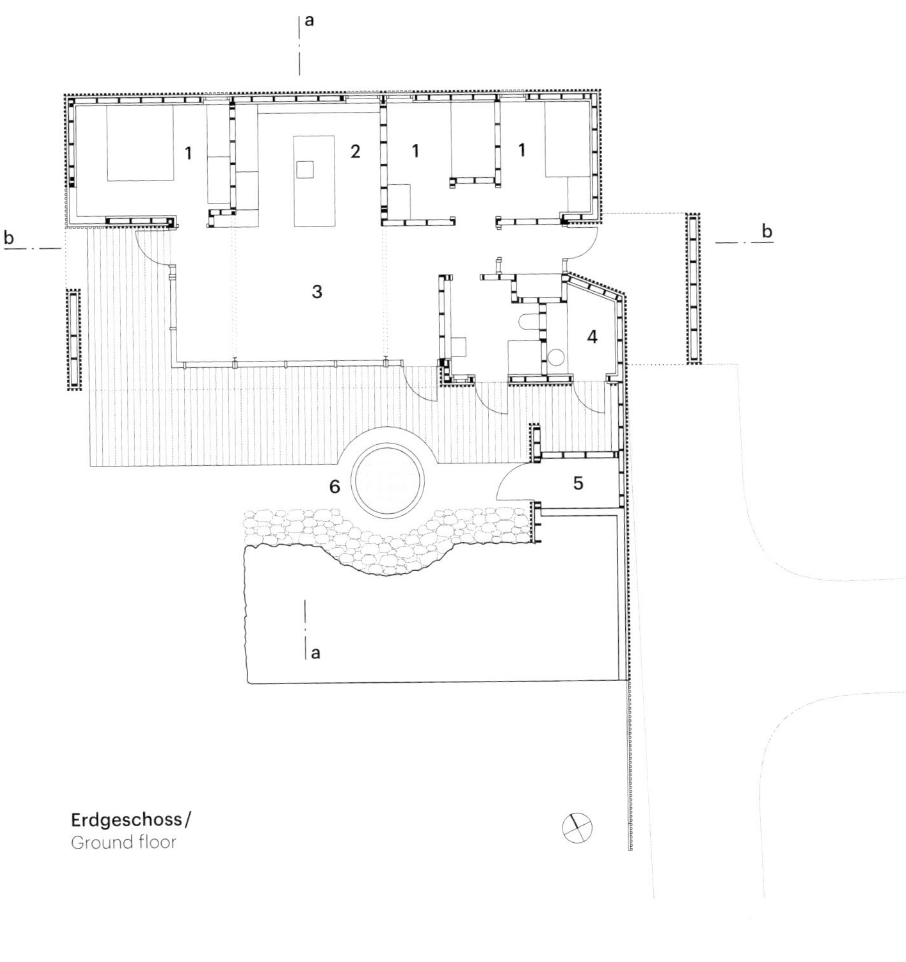

Erdgeschoss /
Ground floor

In den Baumwipfeln des atlantischen Regenwalds

Among the treetops of the Atlantic rain forest

Das dreigeschossige Haus liegt wie eine große Plattform inmitten der wuchernden Dschungelvegetation oberhalb der Küstenstadt Guaruja im brasilianischen Bundesstaat São Paulo. Ein großes Holzdeck, das sich den Konturen des Hangs anpasst, bildet gemeinsam mit einem zusätzlichen Kubus das Erdgeschoss. In ihm ist Platz für ein Spielzimmer und das Bedienstetenquartier. Von hier führt eine lange Treppe – belichtet von einer Installation des dänischen Künstlers Ólafur Elíasson – nach oben in die Wohnräume.
Das eigentliche Haus wächst aufgeständert aus dem Hang in den Regenwald und wird von zwei Stützen getragen. Im unteren Geschoss liegen die Schlafräume mit vorgelagerten Balkonen, darüber die Küche mit Wohn- und Essbereich. Den größten Teil des obersten Stockwerks nimmt die Terrasse ein, die den Blick in den Dschungel und über den Atlantik schweifen lässt. Über verschiebbare Glaselemente an drei Seiten lassen sich die Aufenthaltsräume vollständig zum Freibereich öffnen, sodass innen und außen ineinander übergehen. Die wuchernde Vegetation des Regenwalds wird so zu einer Qualität, die den Charakter der Wohnräume bestimmt.

Architekten: Studio mk27, Marcio Kogan, Samanta Cafardo, Diana Radomysler
Bauherr: privat
Tragwerksplanung: leão associados – eng. João Rubens Leão
Landschaftsarchitektur: Isabel Duprat
Material: Beton, Glas, Holz
Region/Land: Guarujá, São Paulo, Brasilien
Funktion: Ferienhaus
Nutzung: permanent

Like a big platform, the three-storey house is located in the middle of dense jungle vegetation north of the coastal city of Guarujá in the Brazilian State of São Paulo. Together with an additional rectangular volume, a large wooden deck adapted to the contours of the slope forms the ground floor.
A playroom and domestic staff quarters are accommodated in this volume. From there, a long staircase – illuminated by an installation by the Danish artist Ólafur Elíasson – leads to the living space above. The house itself extends out of the slope towards the rain forest supported by two columns. The lower storey contains the bedrooms with projecting balconies, while the kitchen with living and dining area are located above. Most of the upper storey is occupied by a terrace allowing a view of the jungle and across the Atlantic Ocean. Sliding glass elements on three sides make it possible to fully open up the common rooms to the outside, making the transition between indoors and outdoors seamless. The exuberant vegetation of the rain forest becomes a quality that determines the character of the living spaces.

Architects: Studio mk27, Marcio Kogan, Samanta Cafardo, Diana Radomysler
Client: Private
Structural engineering: Leão Associados – Eng. João Rubens Leão
Landscape designer: Isabel Duprat
Material: Concrete, glass, timber
Region/Country: Guarujá, São Paulo, Brazil
Function: Holiday home
Utilisation: Permanent

CASA NA MATA, GUARUJÁ, SÃO PAULO (BR)

Grundrisse / Schnitt
Maßstab 1:400

Floor plans / Section
Scale 1:400

1 Schlafzimmer
2 Terrasse
3 Flur
4 Abstellkammer
5 Essbereich
6 Küche
7 Wohnraum
8 Sauna

1 Bedroom
2 Terrace
3 Hallway
4 Closet
5 Dining area
6 Kitchen
7 Living room
8 Sauna

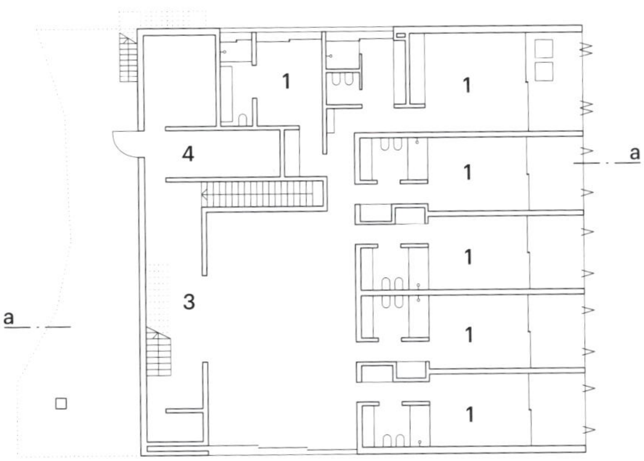

Erdgeschoss/
Ground floor

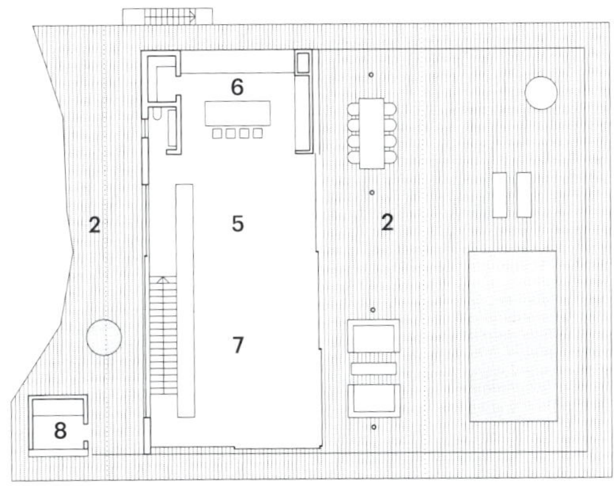

Obergeschoss/
First floor

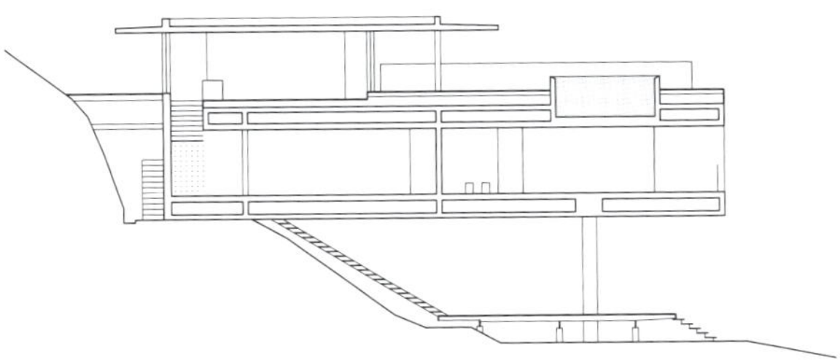

aa

Schutzhütte im Okstindan-Gebirgsmassiv

Mountain refuge in the Okstindan mountain range

Der norwegische Trekking-Verband unterhält zahlreiche Unterkünfte quer durch das ganze Land. Eine davon ist die Rabot Tourist Cabin auf 1200 Metern in der Nähe des Okstindan-Gletschers. Das Wetter kann in dieser Gegend im Norden Norwegens extrem unwirtlich sein – mit viel Schnee und schweren Stürmen. Deshalb entwarfen die Architekten aus Oslo einen schlichten, aerodynamischen Baukörper, der den Elementen kaum Angriffsfläche bietet. Zwei Kamine, die in Analogie zu den dahinterliegenden Gipfeln nach oben ragen, weisen weithin sichtbar den Weg zur Unterkunft, die nach dem französischen Glaziologen Charles Rabot benannten ist. Ihr Äußeres ist mit Fichtenholz verschalt, das durch einen Anstrich mit Eisensulfat eine silbergraue Farbe erhält. Wegen der häufigen Schneeverwehungen gibt es zwei gegenüberliegende Eingänge, die den Zugang sichern. Die Hütte bietet Betten für bis zu 30 Personen in sieben Zimmern. Ein zentraler zweigeschossiger Bereich mit Küche und Schlafgalerie gliedert die Innenräume in zwei Teile, die separat beheizt werden können. In den Gemeinschaftsräumen mit hohen Decken erlauben große Fensterflächen weite Blicke in die raue Natur der Bergkette.

The Norwegian Trekking Association operates many cabins across the whole country. One of these is the Rabot Tourist Cabin near the Okstindan glacier, located at an altitude of 1,200 metres. The weather in this part of northern Norway can be extremely tough – with lots of snow and heavy storms. That's why the architects from Oslo designed a simple, aerodynamic structure offering little opportunity for the aggressive elements to act. Two chimneys, rising upwards in analogy to the peaks beyond, are clearly visible indicators of the route to the lodging, which is named after the French glaciologist Charles Rabot. The exterior is clad with spruce, rendered silver-grey by means of a iron sulphate coating. Two entrances located opposite to each other ensure access to the shelter in an area where snowdrifts are not uncommon. The cabin offers space for up to 30 persons in seven rooms. A central two-storey area with a kitchen and sleeping mezzanine divides the interior into two parts that can be heated separately. Large windows in the high-ceilinged common rooms permit extensive views of the rough nature of the mountain range.

Architekten: Jarmund / Vigsnæs Arkitekter
Bauherr: Hemnes Turistforening
Tragwerksplanung: Walter Jacobsen MNT
Brandschutz: Rambøll
Material: Kiefer (Holz), Stahlbeton
Region / Land: Nordland, Norwegen
Funktion: Schutzhütte
Nutzung: temporär

Architects: Jarmund / Vigsnæs Arkitekter
Client: Hemnes Turistforening
Structural engineering: Walter Jacobsen MNT
Fire: Rambøll
Material: Pine (timber), concrete
Region / Country: Nordland, Norway
Function: Tourist mountain cabin
Utilisation: Temporary

Grundrisse / Schnitte
Maßstab 1:250

1 Eingang
2 Trockentoilette
3 Essbereich
4 Küche
5 Wohnraum
6 Schlafraum
7 Lager
8 Holzlager
9 Luftraum
10 Galerie
11 Etagenbett
12 Technik

Floor plans / Sections
Scale 1:250

1 Entrance
2 Dry toilet
3 Dining room
4 Kitchen
5 Living room
6 Bedroom
7 Storage
8 Wood store
9 Void
10 Mezzanine
11 Bunk bed
12 Services

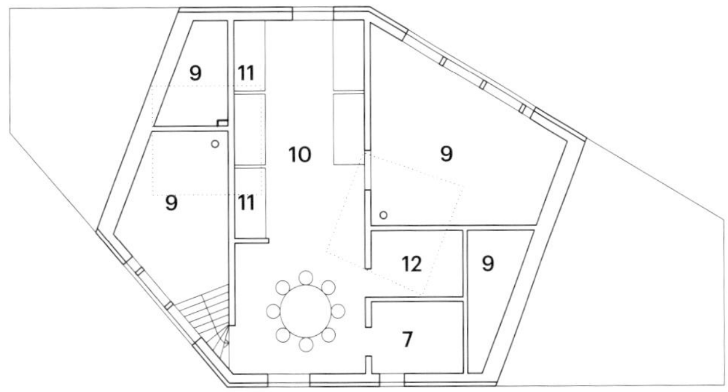

Obergeschoss /
First floor

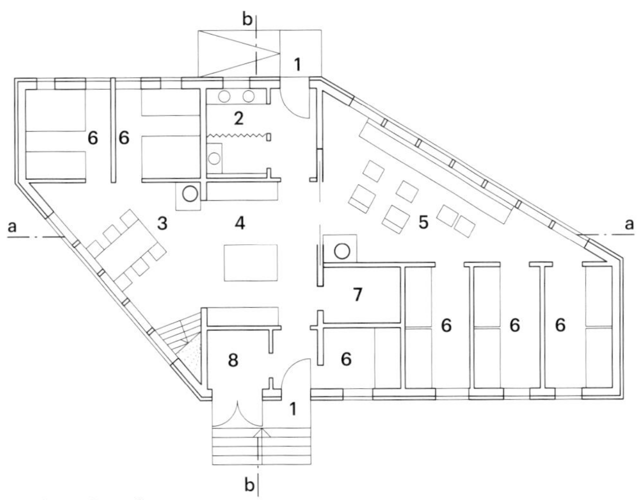

Erdgeschoss /
Ground floor

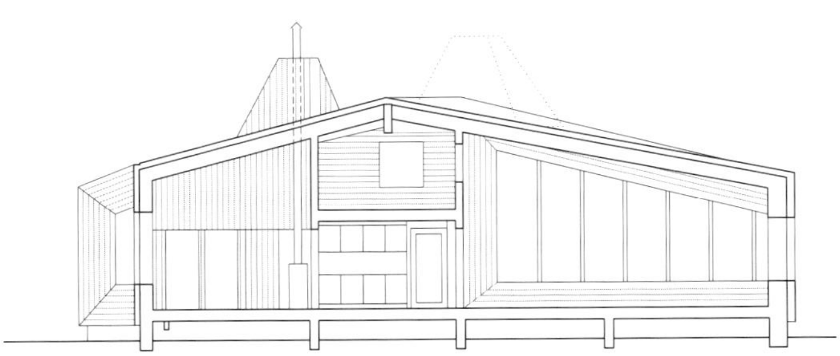

aa

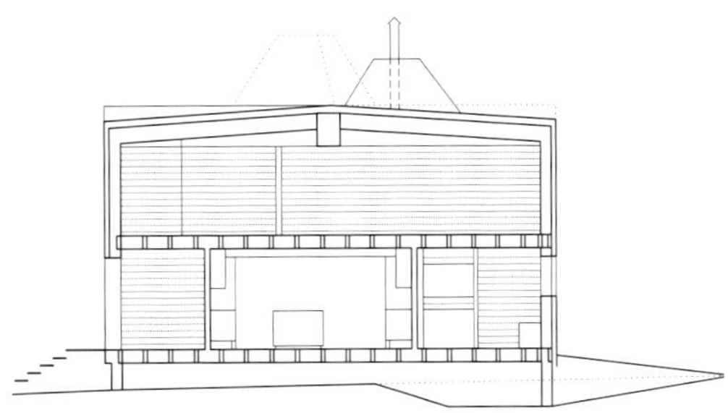

bb

Frontispiz von Marc-Antoine Laugiers »Essai sur l'architecture« (1755) mit einer Darstellung der vitruvianischen Urhütte von Charles Eisen.

Frontispiece of Marc-Antoine Laugier's Essay on Architecture (1755) with an illustration of the vitruvian primitive hut by Charles Eisen.

Von der Subsistenzwirtschaft zur Sommerresidenz

Eine kurze Geschichte des Wohnens auf dem Land

From subsistence economy to summer residence

A short history of living in the country

Jakob Schoof

Warum ziehen Menschen aufs Land – und das freiwillig? Die Frage mag sich nach dem Unverständnis überzeugter Städter anhören, historisch betrachtet ist sie jedoch durchaus von Interesse. Bis zum Beginn des Eisenbahnzeitalters im frühen 19. Jahrhundert waren alle menschlichen Ansiedlungen eng vom Agrarraum in ihrer unmittelbaren Umgebung abhängig. In den Städten der Frühzeit, beispielsweise in Mesopotamien, waren die Bewohner meist auch auf den Feldern tätig, um für ihren Lebensunterhalt zu sorgen.

LANDWIRTSCHAFT UND LANDLUXUS: DAS LEBEN IN DER ANTIKE

Schon in der Antike setzte sich jedoch eine stärkere Arbeitsteilung zwischen Stadt- und Landbevölkerung durch. In den römischen Provinzen umgab ein engmaschiges Netz von mittelgroßen Gutshöfen die Städte und ihre Befestigungsanlagen und versorgte sie mit Nahrungsmitteln. Die meisten dieser als »villae rusticae« bezeichneten Landgüter waren mindestens 25 Hektar groß und befanden sich im Besitz pensionierter Legionäre. Deren Lebensstandard kam demjenigen der städtischen Mittelschicht gleich; ein Landleben ohne Landwirtschaft war für diese Gutsbesitzer gleichwohl undenkbar.
Im 1. und 2. Jahrhundert v. Chr. entwickelte sich in Italien und in einigen neu hinzugekommenen Provinzen des römischen Reichs ein System aus Latifundien (Großgrundbesitzen). Sie spezialisierten sich – neben den landwirtschaftlichen Gütern zur Versorgung von Besitzern und Arbeitskräften – zunehmend auf lukrative Erzeugnisse wie zum Beispiel Wein und Oliven. Ihre Eigentümer, zumeist Senatoren oder andere Patrizier, schufen eine Sonderform der »villa«, die bereits starke Parallelen zu neuzeitlichen Formen des gehobenen Landlebens aufwies: Die »villae urbanae« waren luxuriöse Zweit-, Dritt- oder Viertwohnsitze, die der Repräsentation und der Erholung dienten. »Otium« als Gegenpol zu »negotium«, die Muße auf dem Land als Gegensatz zu den Geschäften in der Stadt, war in den »villae urbanae« zu Hause. Cicero soll mindestens sieben solcher Landsitze besessen haben, obwohl er noch nicht einmal zu den reichsten Männern der römischen Republik gehörte. Noch heute bedeutet der italienische Begriff »villeggiatura« so viel wie »Sommerfrische«.

PIONIERGEMEINSCHAFTEN UND EINSAME EREMITEN: DIE MÖNCHSORDEN DES MITTELALTERS

Im Mittelalter übernahmen allmählich die Klöster die Rolle als geistige Zentren Europas. Sie fungierten oft als Vorposten der Zivilisation und waren im ländlichen Raum angesiedelt. Viele von ihnen gelangten im Laufe der Zeit durch Schenkungen, aber auch durch fortschrittliche Methoden in der Landwirtschaft zu erstaunlichem Reichtum und großem Grundbesitz.
Pioniere für diese Entwicklung waren die Zisterzienser. Der Orden bewegte sich im Spannungsfeld zwischen individueller Armut und kollektivem Wohlstand. Die Prachtentfaltung und der reiche Bauschmuck anderer Ordensgemeinschaften waren den Zisterziensern jedoch fremd. Stattdessen errichteten sie puristische Steinbauten, die auch im 20. Jahrhundert noch viele Architekten begeisterten – darunter Le Corbusier, der sich von ihnen zum Entwurf des Dominikanerklosters La Tourette bei Lyon inspirieren ließ.

ZWISCHEN IDEALISMUS UND PRAGMATISMUS: DIE VILLEN DER RENAISSANCE

Private Wohnformen auf dem Land, die Ähnlichkeiten mit den »villae« der Antike besaßen, etablierten sich erst in der italienischen Renaissance wieder. In den Außenbezirken von Rom ließen Päpste, Kardinäle und Adlige ihre Sommerresidenzen bauen, die bis heute den Nukleus größerer Stadtparks bilden. Zu den bekanntesten Beispielen gehören das Casino der Villa Borghese (1613–1616) und die Villa Doria Pamphili (1644–1652). Tivoli entwickelte sich im 16. Jahrhundert zu einem Ort der Sommerfrische. Ab 1560 errichtete hier der Kardinal und Vertreter Frankreichs Ippolito d'Este II. seinen Palast, der vor allem aufgrund seiner eindrucksvoll terrassierten Renaissancegärten bekannt wurde.
Weitaus stärker landwirtschaftlich geprägt waren die Landsitze der Adligen und Kaufleute im Veneto, für die der Architekt Andrea Palladio ab etwa 1540 tätig wurde. Besonders offenkundig ist der Doppelcharakter aus Repräsentation und agrarischer Nutzung bei der Villa Emo in Fanzolo bei Treviso, die Palladio ab 1564 für den hochrangigen venezianischen Beamten Leonardo Emo errichtete.
Lang gestreckte »barchesse« – Scheunen, denen

Why do people move to the countryside – voluntarily? This question may sound like the incomprehension expressed by a convinced city dweller, yet it is certainly of interest from a historical point of view. Until the beginning of the railway age in the early 19th century, all human settlements were highly dependent on the farming regions in their immediate environment. It was not uncommon for inhabitants of prehistoric towns, such as Mesopotamia, to also work on the fields to safeguard their livelihoods.

AGRICULTURE AND COUNTRY LUXURY: LIFE IN ANCIENT TIMES

A greater differentiation between the work performed by rural and urban populations started to emerge in classical antiquity. Cities and military forts in the Roman provinces were supplied with food through a dense network of medium-sized farms surrounding them. Most of these estates, called "villae rusticae", were at least 25 hectares in size and owned by pensioned legionaries. Their standard of living was similar to that of the urban middle class, yet life in the country without agriculture was inconceivable for these landholders. In the 1st and 2nd centuries BC, a system based on" latifundia" (large agricultural estates) was developed in Italy as well as in several newly conquered provinces. Apart from agricultural produce for the sustenance of owners and labourers, these increasingly specialised in lucrative products such as wine and olives. Their proprietors – mostly senators or other patricians – created a special type of "villa", which already exhibited clear parallels to contemporary forms of exclusive country living: "villae urbanae" were luxurious second, third or fourth homes serving for representation and recreation. "Otium" rather than "negotium" – leisure in the countryside as opposed to business in the city – is what the "villae urbanae" were intended for. Cicero is said to have owned at least seven of such country seats, although he wasn't even among the richest men of the Roman Republic. Even today, the Italian expression "villeggiatura" means "holiday".

PIONEERING COMMUNITIES AND SECLUDED HERMITS: MONASTIC ORDERS OF THE MIDDLE AGES

In the Middle Ages, monasteries started to become the spiritual and intellectual centres of Europe. They often functioned as outposts of civilisation in rural areas. In the course of time, many of them acquired amazing wealth and extensive landholdings through donations as well as progressive agricultural methods.
The Cistercians were pioneers in this development. The order was at the heart of the conflict between individual poverty and collective prosperity. The grandeur and architectural decoration practised by other orders was alien to the Cistercians. Instead, they built purist stone constructions, which continued to fascinate many architects even in the 20th century – including Le Corbusier as inspiration for the design of the Dominican priory La Tourette near Lyon, for example.

BETWEEN IDEALISM AND PRAGMATISM: THE RENAISSANCE VILLAS

Private dwelling forms in the country, exhibiting similarities to the "villae" of ancient times, only became popular again during the Italian Renaissance. Popes, cardinals and noblemen had their summer residences built on the outskirts of Rome and these form the nucleus of larger city parks to this day. The most famous examples include the Casino of the Villa Borghese (1613–1616) and the Villa Doria Pamphili (1644–1652). In the 16th century, Tivoli also developed into a place to spend the summer holidays. Cardinal and governor Ippolito d'Este started to build his palace – primarily renowned for its impressive terraced Renaissance gardens – in Tivoli in 1560.
The country seats of noblemen and merchants in the Veneto, for whom the architect Andrea Palladio was commissioned from about 1540 onwards, had a more agricultural quality. The dual character of representation and agricultural use is particularly obvious in the Villa Emo in Fanzolo near Treviso, which Palladio built for the Venetian patrician Leonardo Emo starting in 1564. Long "barchesse" – barns endowed with a representative exterior through arcades – flank the compact residential space on either side. A broad ramp, leading frontally to the loggia in the piano nobile, is not likely to have served as an accessway for carriages, being too steep and ribbed across. It probably functioned as an inclined threshing floor, on which – facing exactly south – grain could be dried in the sun.[1] Palladio's villas mainly became famous through

Palladio durch Arkaden ein repräsentativeres Äußeres verlieh – flankieren den kompakten Wohntrakt zu beiden Seiten. Die breite Rampe, die frontal auf die Loggia im Piano nobile zuführt, ist als Wagenvorfahrt zu steil und außerdem von Querrillen durchzogen. Sie diente wohl als schräg gestellter Dreschplatz, auf dem das Getreide – genau nach Süden ausgerichtet – in der Sonne trocknen konnte.[1]
Bekannt wurden Palladios Villen vor allem durch die Zeichnungen, die der Architekt in seinen »Quattro libri dell'architettura« veröffentlichte. Als Idealvorstellungen stimmten sie indes selten mit der gebauten Version überein. Das gilt auch für Palladios berühmtesten Villenbau, die Villa Rotonda rund zwei Kilometer südlich von Vicenza. Geplant war sie ursprünglich für den Kleriker Paolo Almerico, der wenig Sinn für Landwirtschaft hatte. Noch vor Baufertigstellung starben sowohl der Bauherr als auch sein Architekt, und Palladios Schüler Vicenzo Scamozzi stellte La Rotonda für das Brüderpaar Odorico und Mauro Carpa fertig. Dabei gestaltete er das Anwesen so um, dass es als Landwirtschaftsbetrieb nutzbar wurde: An der Zufahrt zum Gelände entstand eine Remise für landwirtschaftliches Gerät und – um die Warenanlieferung zu erleichtern – in der Mitte jeder der vier großen Freitreppen eine Durchfahrt, die direkt in das Sockelgeschoss führte.
Im 18. Jahrhundert wurden die Durchfahrten wieder geschlossen, das Hauptgebäude entspricht heute weitgehend Palladios Originalentwurf. Auf einer leichten Anhöhe am Fuße des Monte Berico gelegen, dominiert es die umliegende Flussebene – ein gebautes Symbol für die Landschaftsbeherrschung in der Renaissance.

ZÄHMUNG DER NATUR UND KUNSTLANDSCHAFTEN: GARTENANLAGEN DES 18. JAHRHUNDERTS

Die Neuordnung der Landschaft nach geometrischen Prinzipien kam ein gutes Jahrhundert später in den Barockgärten nördlich der Alpen zur Entfaltung. Anlagen wie Vaux-le-Vicomte und Versailles in Frankreich oder Kassel-Wilhelmshöhe in Deutschland waren ingenieurtechnische Meisterleistungen. Die Landschaft wurde topografisch komplett überformt und von kilometerlangen Kanälen durchzogen, um die kunstvollen Wasserspiele in den Gartenanlagen zu versorgen. Auch die Landschaftsgärten, die sich als bewusster Kontrast zu den barocken Gartenanlagen bald nach 1700 in England und ab Mitte des 18. Jahrhunderts auch in Frankreich durchsetzten, basierten auf fortschrittlicher Ingenieurtechnik. Sie kaschierten diese jedoch mit einem Gewand künstlich erzeugter Ursprünglichkeit, das sich auch in den idealtypischen Landschaften zeitgenössischer Maler wie Claude Lorrain oder Gaspard Poussin wiederfindet. Passend dazu begannen die Adligen jener Zeit, ihre Landschaftsgärten nicht nur mit von der Antike inspirierten Tempelchen und Brücken auszustatten, sondern auch mit pittoresken Urhütten aller Art. Nicht selten ließen sie diese Eremitagen sogar von bezahlten Einsiedlern bewohnen. Die jahrhundertealte christliche Tradition kontemplativer Einsamkeit und Einfachheit wurde damit zum Bestandteil höfischer Unterhaltungskultur.
Auch die bäuerliche Landwirtschaft hielt, zur Lustbarkeit des Adels transformiert, in den Parkanlagen des ausgehenden 18. Jahrhunderts Einzug. Ab 1782 ließ sich die französische Königin Marie-Antoinette im Schlosspark von Versailles das »Hameau de la Reine« (Weiler der Königin) errichten, eine Gebäudegruppe mit Bauernhaus, Mühle, Molkerei, Fischerhütte und Aussichtsturm in Form eines Leuchtturms am Seeufer.
Das Dörfchen war Schau- und Erlebnisarchitektur, die es ihrer adligen Besitzerin erlaubte, für ein paar Stunden der höfischen Etikette zu entfliehen und in die Rolle einer einfachen Landbewohnerin zu schlüpfen. An Komfort mangelte es ihr dennoch nicht: Sehr im Gegensatz zum rustikalen Äußeren besaßen die Bauten ein elaboriertes Rokoko-Interieur.

STAFFAGE UND SOZIALES ENGAGEMENT: COTTAGE-KULT IM 19. JAHRHUNDERT

Spätestens mit der Französischen Revolution wurde dem europäischen Adel klar, dass das Bauen auf dem Land nicht nur dem höfischen Vergnügen dienen konnte, sondern auch die Lebensbedingungen der dortigen Bevölkerung verbessern musste. Vor allem in Großbritannien griff ein regelrechter Cottage-Kult um sich, der in eigentümlicher Gleichzeitigkeit alle Klassen der Bevölkerung umfasste.[2]
Wohlhabende Landbesitzer ließen sich pittoreske

the drawings published by the architect in his "Quattro libri dell'architettura", although the built versions hardly ever matched his ideal conceptions. This also applies to Palladio's most famous construction, the Villa Rotonda, located about two kilometres south of Vicenza. It was originally planned for the clergyman Paolo Almerico, who had little interest in agriculture. Both the client and the architect died before its completion, so that Palladio's student Vicenzo Scamozzi ended up completing La Rotonda for the brothers Odorico and Mauro Carpa. He redesigned the property to make it usable for agriculture. An outbuilding for agricultural equipment was placed near the driveway to the grounds, and a passage through the middle of each of the four large outside staircases leading directly to the basement storey was added to make the delivery of goods easier.
The thoroughfares were closed again in the 18th century, with the main building largely corresponding to Palladio's original design again. Situated on a hilltop at the foot of Monte Berico, it dominates the surrounding flood plain – an architectural symbol of the command of the landscape typical of the Renaissance.

TAMING NATURE AND ART LANDSCAPES: 18TH-CENTURY GARDENS

The trend to design landscapes according to geometrical principles evolved a good century later in the Baroque gardens north of the Alps. Gardens like Vaux-le-Vicomte and Versailles in France or Kassel-Wilhelmshöhe in Germany were genuine masterpieces of engineering. The topography was completely remoulded and pervaded with kilometres-long channels to supply the artistic fountains in the gardens.
Forming a conscious contrast to the Baroque designs, landscape gardens – established in England soon after 1700 as well as in France starting in the mid-18th century – were also based on advanced engineering methods. These were, however, concealed behind an artificially produced naturalness also found in ideal landscapes by contemporary painters like Claude Lorrain or Gaspard Poussin. In line with this, the aristocrats of the time had their landscape gardens populated with small temples and bridges inspired by ancient times and fitted with all kinds of picturesque primitive huts, not seldom inhabited by a paid hermit. The centuries-old Christian tradition of contemplative solitude and simplicity became a component of courtly entertainment culture in this way.
Peasant agriculture – transformed for the amusement of the aristocracy – was also introduced to the parks of the early 18th century. The Queen of France, Marie-Antoinette, had an "Hameau de la Reine" (Hamlet of the Queen) – consisting of a farm house, mill, dairy, fisher hut and lookout in the form of a lighthouse on the shores of the lake – built in the palace gardens of Versailles starting in 1782. The architecture of the little village was for show as well as for use, allowing the royal owner to escape from courtly etiquette for some hours and slip into the role of a simple countrywoman. She did not, however, have to do without comfort: in contrast to their rustic exterior, the buildings were finished with an elaborate rococo interior.

DECORATION AND SOCIAL COMMITMENT: COTTAGE CULT IN THE 19TH CENTURY

No later than by the French Revolution, did the European nobility come to realise that building in the country could not solely serve for courtly entertainment, but also had to improve the living conditions of the local population.[2] A veritable cottage cult developed particularly in Great Britain, which in peculiar simultaneity encompassed all classes of the population. Wealthy landowners had picturesque "cottages ornés" (ornamental cottages) built to indulge in an apparently simple country life. Others, who were offended by the appearance of the existing farmhand dwellings located on their property, had these removed and built anew. On the one hand, this served to keep the landscape looking "neat" in accordance with artistic principles, while on the other hand also improving the living standards of the local population. Some of the new constructions had a reduced, serial look, such as the farmworker settlements in Nuneham Courtenay near Oxford (1761) and Milton Abbas in Dorset (1773–1786), while others displayed an undisguised medieval nostalgia. The uppermost design objective in every case was, however, something described by the English landscape architect Humphry Repton as "simplicité soignée" (well-kept simplicity).

»cottages ornés« (Schmuck-Cottages) errichten, um dort dem scheinbar einfachen Landleben zu frönen. Andere, denen das Erscheinungsbild der bestehenden Landarbeitersiedlungen auf ihrem Grund und Boden ein Dorn im Auge war, ließen diese abtragen und neu errichteten. Das diente einerseits dem Erhalt eines »gepflegten« Landschaftsbilds nach künstlerischen Prinzipien, verbesserte aber andererseits auch den Wohnstandard der dort ansässigen Bevölkerung. Teils hatten die Neubauten ein reduziertes, serielles Erscheinungsbild wie etwa die Landarbeitersiedlungen in Nuneham Courtenay bei Oxford (1761) und Milton Abbas in Dorset (1773–1786), teils sprach aus ihnen unverhohlene Mittelalter-Nostalgie. Oberstes gestalterisches Ziel war aber in jedem Fall, was der englische Landschaftsarchitekt Humphry Repton als »simplicité soignée« (gepflegte Einfachheit) bezeichnete.

STADTFLUCHT I: ARTS AND CRAFTS UND DIE GARTENSTADTBEWEGUNG

Die Cottage-Mode und die Suche nach ursprünglicher Einfachheit zogen sich wie ein roter Faden durch die britische Wohnarchitektur des 19. Jahrhunderts. Sie fielen auf fruchtbaren ideologischen Boden, als sich Entwicklungen gegen die zunehmende Verstädterung zu formieren begannen. Vor allem in der Arts-and-Crafts-Bewegung gingen mittelalterliche Vorbilder und antiurbane Tendenzen ab den 1860er-Jahren eine erfolgreiche Synthese ein. Hinzu kamen bei John Ruskin und seinem Schüler William Morris, den beiden Vordenkern der Bewegung, starke sozialreformerische Bestrebungen.

1859 entwarf Morris gemeinsam mit seinen Architekten- und Künstlerfreunden Philipp Webb und Edward Burne-Jones die Einrichtung und Ausstattung für das Red House in Bexleyheath, südöstlich von London. Das verklinkerte Wohnhaus (daher der Name) gilt als Initialzündung der Arts-and Crafts-Bewegung, hatte mit seinem Charakter als Gesamtkunstwerk aber auch großen Einfluss auf die spätere Jugendstil- und Sezessionsarchitektur. »Abgesehen von dem Wunsch, schöne Dinge herzustellen, ist die dominierende Leidenschaft meines Lebens der Hass auf die moderne Zivilisation«, schrieb Morris 1896.[3] Ironischerweise musste er jedoch dem idyllischen Landleben im Red House bereits 1864 den Rücken kehren, um seine zunehmend florierenden Möbel- und Tapetenwerkstätten in London zu beaufsichtigen.

Morris' künstlerisches Programm wurde überwiegend von Menschen umgesetzt, die mit seinen politischen Ansichten wenig anzufangen wussten. Arts-and-Crafts-Architekten wie C. R. Ashbee, Norman Shaw oder William Lethaby errichteten Landhäuser für die begüterten Schichten. Auch reiche Mäzene griffen den Trend zur Stadtflucht auf: Ab 1888 errichtete der Seifenfabrikant William Hesketh Lever bei Liverpool die Siedlung Port Sunlight und ermöglichte es seinen Fabrikarbeitern so, der schlechten Luft der nordenglischen Industriemetropole zu entkommen. Ab 1893 folgte der Schokoladenhersteller George Cadbury mit seiner Modellsiedlung Bournville vor den Toren von Birmingham. Ziel des Vorhabens war es, die »Übel der modernen, engen Lebensverhältnisse zu mildern«.

Wie schon die Arts-and-Crafts-Bewegung konnte sich der große Propagandist der Gartenstadt, Ebenezer Howard, daher auf eine breite Palette an Anschauungsmaterial stützen, als er seine Ideen 1902 in dem Buch »Garden Cities of To-Morrow« publizierte. Howards Werk lässt sich am ehesten als retroaktives Manifest interpretieren, das für eine sich bereits abzeichnende Bewegung das theoretische Fundament schuf.

Zur Verwirklichung seiner Ideen wurde Howard von Cadbury, Lever und anderen Industriemäzenen finanziell unterstützt. 1899 entstand in England die Garden City Association, und schon bald nahmen die ersten Gartenstädte Gestalt an: Letchworth (1904) und Welwyn Garden City (1920) in Großbritannien sowie Dresden-Hellerau, Essen-Margarethenhöhe (beide ab 1909) und die Nürnberger Gartenstadt (1910) in Deutschland. Keine der Neugründungen war jedoch als eigenständige Gartenstadt konzipiert; stets handelte es sich um Vorstadtsiedlungen bestehender Großstädte. Immerhin wurden wesentliche Eckpunkte von Howards Programmatik wie die genossenschaftliche Organisation und eine Selbstversorgung mit eigenen Lebensmittelläden darin in aller Regel verwirklicht.

URBAN FLIGHT I: ARTS AND CRAFTS AND THE GARDEN CITY MOVEMENT

The cottage style and a quest for natural simplicity were the central themes of 19th-century British domestic architecture. This was fostered by a developing ideology against increasing urbanisation. Particularly in the Arts and Crafts movement, medieval models and anti-urban tendencies engaged in a fruitful synthesis starting in the 1860s. This was compounded by considerable ambitions regarding social reform propagated by John Ruskin and his student William Morris, the two thought leaders of the movement.

Together with his architect and artist friends Philipp Webb and Edward Burne-Jones, Morris designed the fittings and furnishings of the Red House in Bexleyheath, south-east of London. The residential brick house (hence its name) is considered the initial spark of the Arts and Crafts movement, its character as an overall work of art also exerting considerable influence on art nouveau and secession architecture later. Morris wrote in 1896: "Apart from the desire to produce beautiful things, the leading passion of my life has been and is hatred of modern civilization."[3] Ironically, he had to leave the idyllic country life in the Red House early in order to supervise his increasingly successful furniture and wallpaper workshops in London in 1864.

Morris's artistic programme was predominantly implemented by people who did not really relate to his political views. Arts and Crafts architects such as C. R. Ashbee, Norman Shaw or William Lethaby built country houses for the wealthy classes. Numerous rich patrons also responded to the urban flight trend: soap manufacturer William Hesketh Lever started to build Port Sunlight in 1888. This settlement near Liverpool allowed his factory workers to escape from the bad air of the north English industrial centre. The chocolate manufacturer George Cadbury followed suit in 1893 with his model settlement Bournville outside Birmingham. The aim was to "alleviate the evils of modern, more cramped living conditions".

As the Arts and Crafts movement before, the great propagandist of the garden city, Ebenezer Howard, was therefore able to make use of a broad range of illustrative material when he published his ideas in the book "Garden Cities of To-morrow" in 1902. Howard's work can best be interpreted as a retroactive manifesto creating a theoretical foundation for the movement that was already beginning to emerge.

Howard was financially supported in the realisation of his ideas by Cadbury, Lever and other industrial patrons. The Garden City Association was established in England in 1899, with the first garden cities starting to develop soon afterwards: Letchworth (1904) and Welwyn Garden City (1920) in Great Britain as well as Dresden-Hellerau, Essen-Margarethenhöhe (both from 1909 onwards) and Nuremberg's Gartenstadt (1910) in Germany. None of the new foundations was, however, designed as an independent garden city, each of them being residential areas located in the suburbs of existing large cities. Significant elements of Howard's objectives, such as cooperative organisation and self-sufficiency with own grocery stores, were nevertheless generally realised.

URBAN FLIGHT II: HEALING NATURE

Modern health tourism is also rooted in the urban flight of the 19th century. It first came about when more and more people living in big overpopulated cities fell prey to contagious diseases. A large number of deaths was attributable alone to tuberculosis at the beginning of the 19th century. Attempts to relieve the symptoms of the lung disease were made for a long time by staying in the country, albeit without much success. The first lung sanatorium in the world was founded by a German doctor called Hermann Brehmer, in the Silesian mountain village of Görbersdorf in 1854. Davos was the first institution of this kind in the Alps in 1862, while Edward Livingston Trudeau had a cottage-style sanatorium built in the Adirondack Mountains north of New York in 1885. Climatic Alpine spas renowned for their beneficial air particularly turned into veritable pilgrimage places for members of the middle classes suffering from tuberculosis. Between 1903 and 1940, a real sanatorium industry with 18 houses for a total of 1,500 patients was established by the Swiss doctor Auguste Rollier in Leysin, high above Lake Geneva. In the decades that followed, the Queen Alexandra sanatorium in Davos – a reinforced concrete structure with projecting, south-facing balconies designed by the architects Otto Pfleghard and

STADTFLUCHT II: DIE HEILENDE NATUR

Auch der moderne Gesundheitstourismus hat seine historischen Wurzeln in der Stadtflucht des 19. Jahrhunderts. Seine Geburtsstunde schlug, als immer mehr Menschen in den überbevölkerten Großstädten ansteckenden Krankheiten zum Opfer fielen. Allein auf die Tuberkulose ging Anfang des 19. Jahrhunderts eine große Zahl aller Todesfälle zurück. Lange Zeit – und letztlich wenig erfolgreich – versuchte man, die Symptome der Lungenkrankheit durch einen Aufenthalt auf dem Land zu lindern. 1854 gründete der deutsche Arzt Hermann Brehmer das erste Lungensanatorium der Welt im schlesischen Bergdorf Görbersdorf. 1862 entstand in Davos die erste Einrichtung dieser Art im Alpenraum, und 1885 ließ Edward Livingston Trudeau in den Adirondack Mountains nördlich von New York ein Sanatorium im Cottage-Stil errichten. Vor allem die Luftkurorte der Alpen avancierten zu wahren Pilgerstätten des tuberkulosegeplagten Bürgertums. In Leysin oberhalb des Genfer Sees zog der Schweizer Arzt Auguste Rollier zwischen 1903 und 1940 eine wahre Sanatorienindustrie mit 18 Häusern für insgesamt 1500 Patienten auf. In Davos wurde das Sanatorium Queen Alexandra der Architekten Otto Pfleghard und Max Haefeli – ein Stahlbetonbau mit ausladenden, zur Südsonne ausgerichteten Balkonen – zum Modell für die Sanatoriumsbauten

WALDEN;

OR,

LIFE IN THE WOODS.

BY HENRY D. THOREAU,

AUTHOR OF "A WEEK ON THE CONCORD AND MERRIMACK RIVERS."

I do not propose to write an ode to dejection, but to brag as lustily as chanticleer in the morning, standing on his roost, if only to wake my neighbors up. — Page 92.

BOSTON:

TICKNOR AND FIELDS.

M DCCC LIV.

Titelbild der ersten Ausgabe von Henry David Thoreau's »Walden«, veröffentlicht 1854 in den USA bei Ticknor and Fields.

Title page from the first edition of Henry David Thoreau's Walden, published in 1854 in the United States by Ticknor and Fields

Ebenezer Howard, Propagandist der Gartenstadt, publizierte seine Ideen in dem Buch »Garden Cities of To-Morrow, A Peaceful Path to Real Reform«, London, Swan Sonnenschein, 1898.

Ebenezer Howard, advocate of the garden city, published his ideas in the book, "Garden Cities of To-Morrow", A Peaceful Path to Real Reform, London, Swan Sonnenschein, 1898.

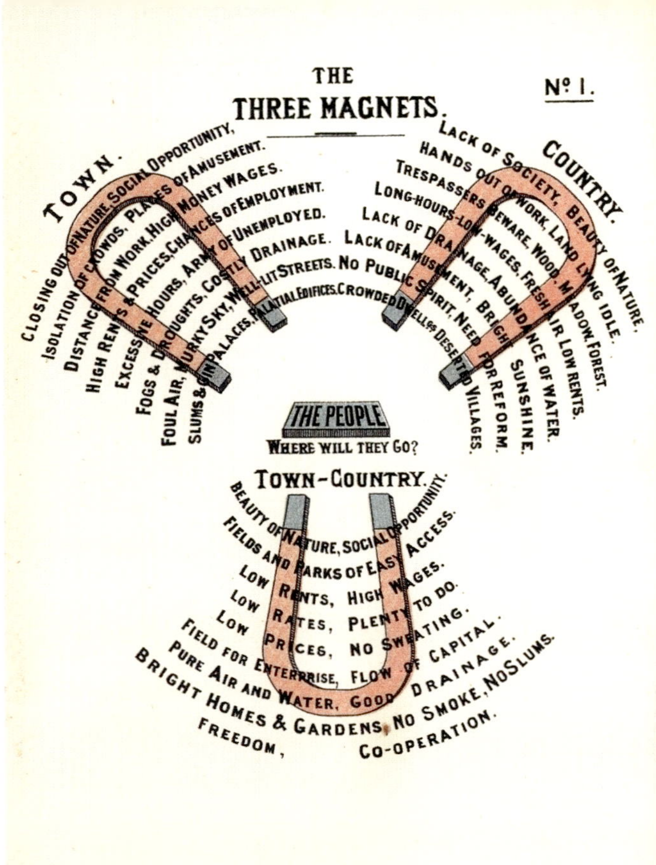

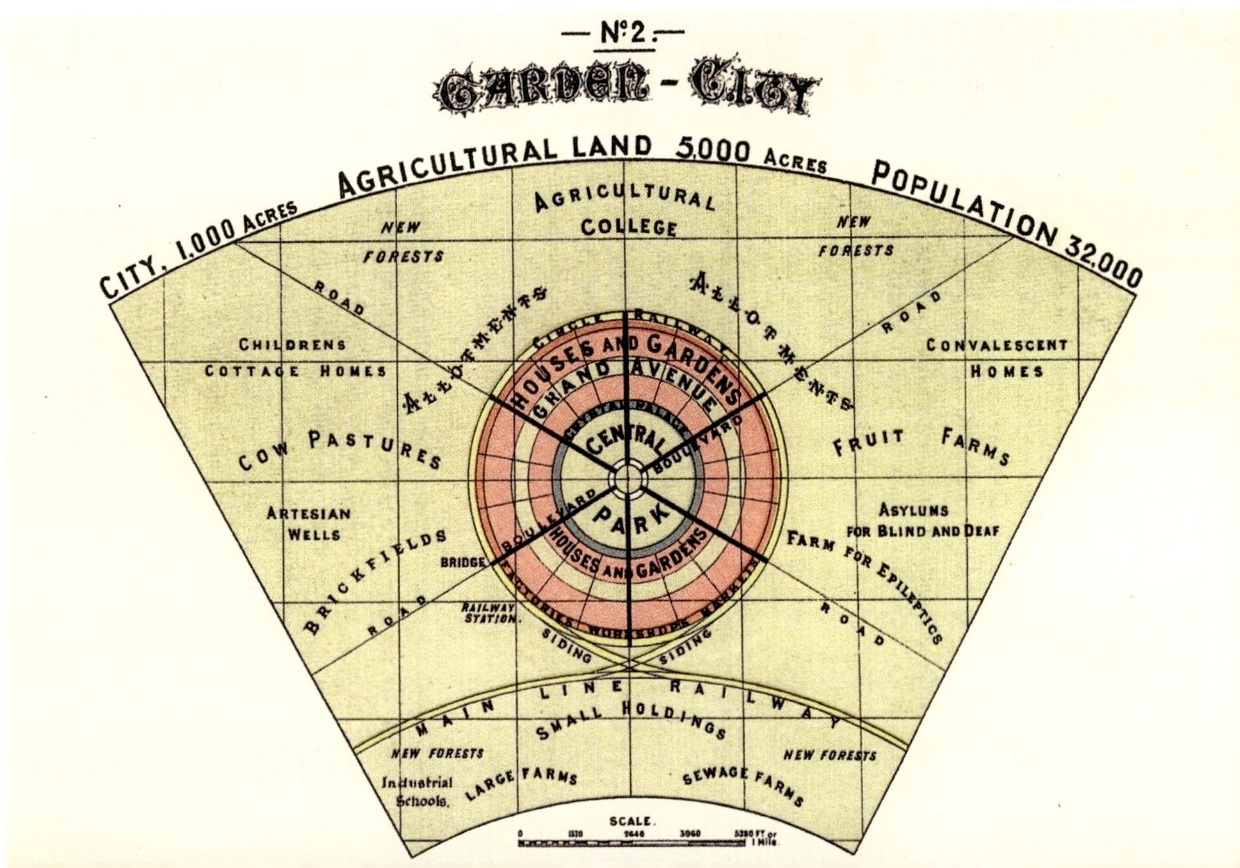

der folgenden Jahrzehnte.[4] Führende europäische Architekten wie Jan Duiker mit dem Sanatorium Zonnestraal bei Hilversum (1926–1931) und Alvar Aalto mit seinem hoch aufragenden Sanatoriumsgebäude im finnischen Paimio (1932) griffen diesen Bautyp in abgewandelter Form auf.
Erst in den 1940er-Jahren gelang es, die ersten Antibiotika gegen Tuberkulose und andere Seuchen in industriellem Maßstab herzustellen. Damit endete auch die Hochzeit der Sanatorien. Der Beliebtheit der Alpen und anderer Bergregionen tat das keinen Abbruch: Inzwischen hatte sich dort der Ski-, Wander- und Gesundheitstourismus fest etabliert.

STADTFLUCHT III: DER RUF DER WILDNIS

1845 erfand der Sohn eines Bleistiftfabrikanten und Harvard-Absolvent Henry David Thoreau seine eigene Version der Stadtflucht: Er zog an den Walden-See unweit der Kleinstadt Concord im US-Bundesstaat Massachusetts und errichtete dort eine 15 Quadratmeter kleine Blockhütte, in der er die beiden darauffolgenden Jahre verbrachte. Thoreau war seinerzeit Privatsekretär des Schriftstellers und Philosophen Ralph Waldo Emerson. Dessen Credo lautete, dass der Mensch einfach und im Einklang mit der Natur leben sollte. Diese Erfahrung strebte Thoreau mit seiner Zivilisationsflucht an. Besonders weit musste er sich dafür nicht bewegen: Der Walden Pond lag nur rund drei Kilometer außerhalb der Stadt, und das Grundstück befand sich im Besitz seines Arbeitgebers. Vermutlich hätte die Nachwelt kaum Notiz von Thoreaus Eremitentum genommen, wenn er darüber nicht sieben Jahre später in seinem Buch »Walden, or Life in the Woods« Zeugnis abgelegt hätte.[5] Seinen Zeitgenossen galt Thoreau als Sonderling. Heute hingegen zählt der mit Reflexionen über die menschliche Zivilisation gespickte Erfahrungsbericht zu den meistrezipierten Werken der US-Literaturgeschichte.

HINAUS NACH SUBURBIA: DIE LANDSCHAFTS-ZERSIEDLUNG DES 20. JAHRHUNDERTS

Gelegentlich wird behauptet, die Korruption der Gartenstadt-Idee durch das Automobil habe geradewegs zum »urban sprawl« des 20. Jahrhunderts geführt. Doch der Wunsch, das Leben

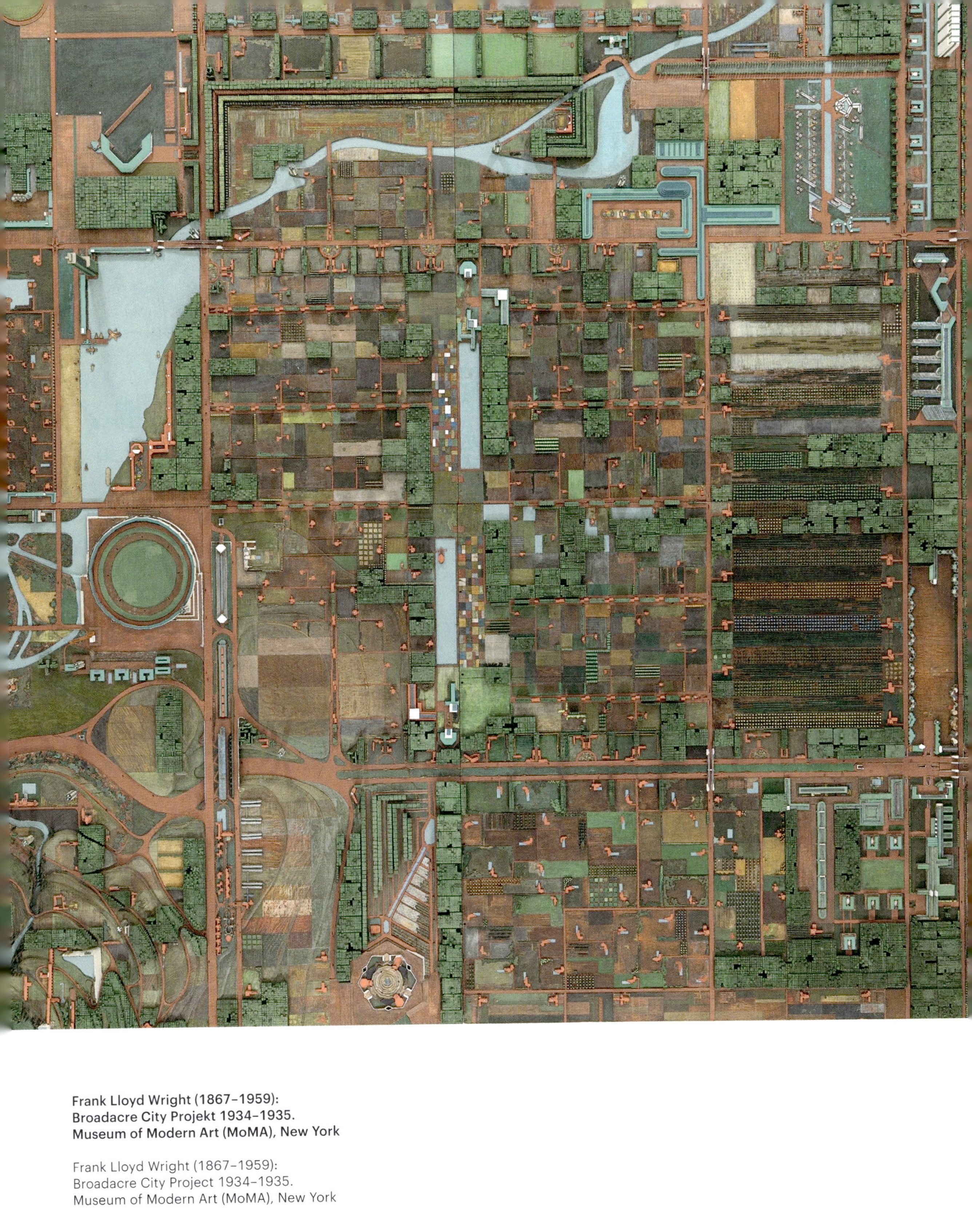

Frank Lloyd Wright (1867–1959):
Broadacre City Projekt 1934–1935.
Museum of Modern Art (MoMA), New York

Frank Lloyd Wright (1867–1959):
Broadacre City Project 1934–1935.
Museum of Modern Art (MoMA), New York

im Grünen mit der Arbeit in der Stadt zu verbinden, reicht weit in das vor-automobile Zeitalter zurück, wie der US-Ökonom Edward Glaeser darlegt.[6] Der Washington Square in New York oder das Eixample von Barcelona, so Glaeser, waren der ausufernde Stadtrand früherer Jahrhunderte, nur dass der Pendlerverkehr damals auf Pferdebussen und der Eisenbahn basierte statt auf Privatautos. 1827 entstand in New York der erste von Pferden gezogene Omnibus, in den 1870er-Jahren die erste dampfbetriebene Hochbahn und 1904 schließlich die elektrische Untergrundbahn. Dennoch wurde ab den 1920er-Jahren das Auto zur größten Triebkraft für die Landschaftszersiedlung. Als Pioniere der Suburbanisierung betätigten sich zum Beispiel der Baumagnat William Levitt und sein Bruder Arthur. In den 1930er-Jahren errichteten sie rund 2000 Wohnhäuser vorwiegend für reiche New Yorker auf Long Island. Etwa zeitgleich publizierte Frank Lloyd Wright erstmals seine utopische Vision von Broadacre City, einer sich endlos ausdehnenden, durchgrünten Stadtlandschaft. Der im ländlichen Mittleren Westen aufgewachsene Wright war wie zuvor William Morris Großstadtskeptiker und Anhänger sozialistischen Gedankenguts. Sehr im Gegensatz etwa zu Le Corbusiers Cité radieuse verstand er Broadacre City nicht als zentral organisiertes, von Architekten durchgeplantes Stadtgefüge, sondern als weitgehend unkontrolliert wachsendes Netzwerk von Straßen, Infrastruktureinrichtungen und Wohnsiedlungen, das sich seiner Überzeugung nach durch das Wirken der Marktkräfte von ganz allein über die USA ausbreiten würde. Die Entwicklung nach dem Zweiten Weltkrieg hat Wrights Prognosen eindrucksvoll bestätigt.

ZWISCHEN WOHNRAUMMANGEL UND FERIENARCHITEKTUR: BAUEN AUF DEM LAND HEUTE

In den letzten Jahren haben in Deutschland vor allem zwei Thesen den Diskurs über das Wohnen auf dem Land dominiert. Beide treffen nur mit Einschränkungen zu. Die erste lautet: Wir erleben eine Reurbanisierung, also eine Rückkehr der Menschen in die Stadt. Tatsächlich zieht es vor allem die unter 30-Jährigen vom Land in die Städte, wenn sie eine Ausbildung beginnen oder eine Arbeitsstelle antreten. Bei allen anderen Altersgruppen muss man stärker differenzieren: Der Außenwanderungssaldo, bei dem die Migration über regionale Grenzen hinweg betrachtet wird, ist für Großstädte auch bei den 30- bis 65-Jährigen positiv. Innerhalb der Ballungsregionen ist der Trend zur Suburbanisierung hingegen bei allen Altersgruppen über 30 ungebrochen. Offenbar hat das Wohnen im Grünen nichts von seiner Attraktivität verloren.[7] Die zweite These besagt, dass ländliche Regionen unter Bevölkerungsschwund, Überalterung sowie einem Mangel an Infrastruktur, Bildungs- und Arbeitsangeboten litten. Dies trifft jedoch in Deutschland längst nicht auf alle Gegenden zu. Vom Saarland bis an die Oder zieht sich ein breiter Streifen schrumpfender ländlicher Regionen durch die Mitte des Landes. In Baden-Württemberg, Bayern, Schleswig-Holstein und dem nördlichen Niedersachsen hingegen verzeichnen viele Landkreise Wirtschaftswachstum und Bevölkerungszuwachs.[8] Hier mangelt es weniger an Arbeitsplätzen als vielmehr an adäquaten Wohnungsangeboten für kinderlose Singles und Paare sowie ältere Menschen. Auf zwei weitere Phänomene weist die britische National Housing Federation in ihrer Broschüre »Rural Housing – Countryside in Crisis« hin:[9] Wohnhäuser auf dem Land haben oft einen wesentlich schlechteren Sanierungszustand als jene in der Stadt, weshalb ihre Bewohner unter einem höheren Armutsrisiko durch hohe Energiekosten leiden. Außerdem ist in vielen ländlichen Regionen ein deutlicher Trend hin zu Zweitwohnsitzen von Stadtbewohnern zu verzeichnen. Für die einheimische Bevölkerung wird es daher zunehmend schwer, bezahlbaren Wohnraum zu finden. Das Problem, das im Alpenraum schon länger beklagt (und dem zunehmend durch eine entsprechende Gesetzgebung begegnet) wird, existiert also offenbar auch im ländlichen Raum in Großbritannien. Damit setzt sich eine Tendenz fort, die bis zur römischen »villa urbana« zurückreicht und die im 20. Jahrhundert architektonische Meisterwerke wie Frank Lloyd Wrights Falling Water, Alvar Aaltos Villa Mairea und Le Corbusiers Villa Savoye hervorgebracht hat. Sie alle waren Wochenendhäuser reicher Städter.

Max Haefeli – was considered a model of sanatorium architecture.[4] Variations of this building type were created by leading European architects such as Jan Duiker with the Zonnestraal sanatorium near Hilversum (1926–1931) and Alvar Aalto with his tall sanatorium constructions in Paimio, Finland (1932). Industrial production of the first antibiotics against tuberculosis and other epidemics finally became possible in the late 1940s, heralding the end of the golden days of the sanatorium. The popularity of the Alps and other mountain regions was not diminished, however, with skiing, hiking and health tourism having become firmly established there in the meantime.

URBAN FLIGHT III: THE CALL OF THE WILD

In the United States, Henry David Thoreau, son of a pencil manufacturer and Harvard graduate, came up with his own version of urban flight in 1845: he moved to Walden Pond close to the small town of Concord in the state of Massachusetts. He spent two consecutive years living in a small log cabin, 15 square meters in size, which he built there. Thoreau was the private secretary of the author and philosopher Ralph Waldo Emerson at the time. The latter's credo was that people should live simply and in harmony with nature. Thoreau was seeking this experience with his flight from civilisation. He didn't have to go far for it: Walden Pond was only about three kilometres outside the city and the plot of land was owned by his employer. Posterity probably would not have taken much note of Thoreau's experience as a recluse, if he hadn't written about it in his book Walden seven years later.[5] Thoreau was considered an eccentric by his contemporaries. Nowadays, his report on the experience filled with reflections on human civilisation is considered one of the most widely read books in the literary history of the United States.

OUT TO SUBURBIA: URBAN SPRAWL OF THE 20TH CENTURY

It is sometimes claimed that corruption of the garden city idea through the motor vehicle led directly to the urban sprawl of the 20th century. Yet the desire to combine living in a green environment with working in the city goes back to far before the age of the automobile, as explained by the US economist Edward Glaeser.[6] According to Glaeser, Washington Square in New York or Eixample in Barcelona, were the sprawl of earlier centuries, with commuters travelling by horse-drawn vehicles and the railway rather than private cars. The first horse-drawn bus was on the road in New York in 1827, the first steam-driven elevated train in the 1870s, finally followed by the electric subway train in 1904. Yet starting in the 1920s, the car became the largest driving force of urban sprawl. William Levitt and his brother Arthur were active pioneers of suburbanisation, for example. They built around 2,000 residential houses, mainly for wealthy New Yorkers, in the 1930s. At about the same time, Frank Lloyd Wright published his utopian vision of Broadacre City, an infinitely extending green city landscape. Like William Morris before him, Wright – who had grown up in the rural Midwest – was sceptical of big cities and a supporter of socialist ideas. Quite contrary to Le Corbusier's Cité Radieuse, for instance, he did not consider Broadacre City to be a centrally organised urban fabric designed by architects. Instead he thought of it as an extensively uncontrolled, growing network of streets, infrastructural facilities and housing developments that he was convinced would spread across the USA solely by the action of market forces. Wright's prognoses were impressively confirmed by developments after World War II.

BETWEEN HOUSING SHORTAGES AND HOLIDAY ARCHITECTURE: BUILDING IN THE COUNTRY TODAY

Two theses have mainly dominated discussions about living in the country in Germany in the past years. Both of them only apply to a limited extent. The first proposes that we are experiencing a reurbanisation – a return of people to the city. Primarily the under-30-year-olds are in fact drawn from rural to urban environments, when they begin training or start work. A greater differentiation must be made with regard to all other age groups. The external migration balance, which considers migration beyond regional borders, is also positive for large cities as far as 30- to 65-year-olds are concerned, yet within urban agglomerations, the trend towards suburbanisation is unbroken for all age groups above 30. Living in a green environment has obviously lost none of its attraction.[7]

DEN MENSCHEN ZULIEBE: STADTNATUR FÜR DAS 21. JAHRHUNDERT

Man braucht nicht viel Fantasie, um zu begreifen, dass luxuriöse Zweitwohnsitze kaum die Lösung sind, um die Lebensbedingungen für bald acht Milliarden Erdbewohner zu verbessern. Gerade in den Metropolen der Welt muss – allen Verdichtungstendenzen zum Trotz – der Zugang zur Natur erhalten bleiben.

Dabei geht es nicht so sehr um den Klima- und Umweltschutz, sondern in erster Linie um die Lebensqualität der Menschen. So absorbieren zum Beispiel sämtliche 26.000 Bäume im New Yorker Central Park gerade einmal so viel CO_2 aus der Luft, wie 37 New Yorker im selben Zeitraum ausstoßen.[10] Für den Erhalt des Klimas ist das ein wenig relevanter Beitrag. Andererseits haben Wissenschaftler in den letzten Jahrzehnten immer neue Effekte entdeckt, wie sich Kontakt zur Natur positiv auf Gesundheit und Wohlbefinden des Menschen auswirkt. Glaubt man ihren Studien, dann beschleunigt der Blick aus dem Fenster hinaus ins Grüne die Genesung nach Operationen in Krankenhäusern und senkt den Bedarf an Schmerzmitteln. Außerdem soll ein Spaziergang im Grünen Stress abbauen und den Blutdruck senken. Eine »grünere« Wohnumgebung kann (unabhängig vom sozialen Status der Kinder) für einen schnelleren Lernfortschritt in der Schule sorgen sowie zu höherer Kreativität und besserem Sozialverhalten bei Kindern führen. Über die Aussagekraft vieler Studien streiten die Experten zwar; in der Summe ergibt sich aus den Untersuchungen jedoch ein eindeutiges Bild: Wem an sozialem Zusammenhalt in der Bevölkerung und funktionierender Gesundheitsvorsorge gelegen ist, sollte öffentliche Gelder nicht nur in Sozialhilfeprogramme und medizinische Forschung investieren, sondern auch die gebaute Umwelt in unseren Städten im Blick behalten. Letztlich geht es um nachhaltige Qualitäten, die den Alltag der Menschen auszeichnen und ihnen den Weg in die Zukunft weisen – sowohl in der Stadt als auch auf dem Land.

1 Martin Kubelik, »Palladio's Villas in the Tradition of the Veneto Farm«, in: Assemblage, 01/1986, S. 90–115
2 vgl. hierzu John Farmer, Green Shift, Oxford 1996.
3 William Morris, Henry Mayers Hyndman, »How I Became a Socialist«, in: Twentieth Century Press, London 1896; morrisedition.lib.uiowa.edu/how-I-became-a-socialist.pdf (Stand 27.11.2017)
4 Paul Overy, Light, Air and Openness. Modern Architecture Between the Wars, London 2007
5 Henry David Thoreau, Walden, or: Life in the Woods, Boston 1854 (deutsche Ausgabe: Walden. Ein Leben mit der Natur, München 1999)
6 Edward Glaeser, Triumph of the City, London 2011
7 Antonia Milbert, Wie viel (Re-)Urbanisierung durchzieht das Land?, BBSR-Analyse Kompakt, 07/2017, Bonn 2017
8 Bundesministerium für Ernährung und Landwirtschaft (Hrsg.), Ländliche Regionen verstehen, Berlin 2016, S. 10
9 National Housing Federation, Rural Housing. Countryside in Crisis, London 2014
10 The Why Factory, Green Dream. How Future Cities Can Outsmart Nature, Rotterdam 2010

The second thesis claims that rural regions are suffering from a population drain, ageing of the population as well as a lack of infrastructure, educational and work opportunities. This does not, however, apply to all regions in Germany. A broad strip of shrinking rural regions crosses the middle of the country from the Saarland to the river Oder. In Baden-Württemberg, Bavaria, Schleswig-Holstein and northern Lower Saxony, on the other hand, many districts report economic growth and rising populations.[8] These regions are short of adequate housing for childless singles and couples as well as for older persons, rather than workplaces. Two further phenomena are pointed out by the British National Housing Federation in its brochure, Rural Housing – Countryside in Crisis.[9] First, houses in the countryside are often in a significantly worse state of repair than those in the city, which is why their occupants are at a higher risk of poverty due to high energy costs. Second, there is moreover a clear trend towards city dwellers having second homes in rural areas. This makes it increasingly difficult for the local population to find affordable living space. The problem, complained about in the Alpine region for some time (and increasingly met by corresponding legislation), obviously also exists in the rural regions of Great Britain. This continues a trend going back to the Roman "villa urbana" which produced 20th-century architectural masterpieces such as Frank Lloyd Wright's Falling Water, Alvar Aalto's Villa Mairea and Le Corbusier's Villa Savoye. All of these were weekend houses belonging to rich city dwellers.

FOR THE SAKE OF HUMANS: URBAN NATURE FOR THE 21ST CENTURY

It doesn't take a lot of imagination to understand that luxurious second homes are hardly the solution for improving the living conditions of the soon eight billion people living on Earth. In spite of all densification trends, access to nature must be retained, particularly in the metropolises of the world.
Of primary concern in this regard is the quality of human life, rather than climate and environmental protection. The 26,000 trees in New York's Central Park, for instance, absorb just about as much CO_2 from the air as is emitted by 37 New Yorkers in the same space of time.[10] As far as climate conservation is concerned, this is an almost negligible amount. On the other hand, scientists keep discovering new ways through which contact to nature has a positive impact on the health and well-being of human beings. According to their studies, a view of greenery from the window accelerates recuperation after surgery in hospitals and decreases the demand for painkillers. A walk in nature furthermore reduces stress and lowers blood pressure. Irrespective of the social status of children, a "greener" living environment can promote faster learning progress at school as well as lead to higher creativity and better social behaviour in children. The significance of many of these studies is debated by experts, yet it seems clear that striving for social cohesion within the population and a functioning preventive health care system, requires more than merely investing in social welfare programmes and medical research: an eye should also be kept on the built environment in our cities. After all, the sustainable qualities characterising the everyday life of human beings and showing them the way forward are what count – both in urban and rural environments.

1 Martin Kubelik, "Palladio's Villas in the Tradition of the Veneto Farm", in: Assemblage, 01/1986, p. 90–115
2 cf. John Farmer, Green Shift, Oxford 1996.
3 William Morris, Henry Mayers Hyndman, "How I Became a Socialist", in: Twentieth Century Press, London 1896; morrisedition.lib.uiowa.edu/how-I-became-a-socialist.pdf (accessed 27.11.2017)
4 Paul Overy, Light, Air and Openness. Modern Architecture Between the Wars, London 2007
5 Henry David Thoreau, Walden, or: Life in the Woods, Boston 1854 (Walden. Ein Leben mit der Natur, München 1999)
6 Edward Glaeser, Triumph of the City, London 2011
7 Antonia Milbert, Wie viel (Re-)Urbanisierung durchzieht das Land? (How much (re-) urbanisation is pervading the country?), BBSR-Analyse Kompakt, 07/2017, Bonn 2017
8 Bundesministerium für Ernährung und Landwirtschaft, Hrsg. (Federal Ministry of Food and Agriculture, publ.), Ländliche Regionen verstehen (Understanding rural regions), Berlin 2016, p. 10
9 National Housing Federation, Rural Housing. Countryside in Crisis, London 2014
10 The Why Factory, Green Dream. How Future Cities Can Outsmart Nature, Rotterdam 2010

SANDRA HOFMEISTER
ist Chefredakteurin von Detail. Nach dem Studium der Kunstgeschichte und Romanistik in Berlin und München promovierte sie an der Ludwig-Maximilians-Universität. Von 2012 bis 2015 war sie Chefredakteurin der deutschen Domus. Ihre Texte mit den Schwerpunkten Architektur und Design sind in internationalen Zeitungen, Zeitschriften und Büchern erschienen. Neben ihrer Tätigkeit als Redakteurin und Herausgeberin ist Sandra Hofmeister Lehrbeauftragte an der Architekturfakultät der Technischen Universität München. Am Wochenende und in den Ferien ist sie meistens in den Bergen oder am Meer. Sandra Hofmeister lebt in München.

JAKOB SCHOOF
ist Redakteur von Detail und verantwortet dort insbesondere die Themenausgaben und -specials zu Energieeffizienz und Nachhaltigkeit. Nach dem Architekturstudium an der Universität Karlsruhe arbeitete er von 2000 bis 2009 bei der Architekturzeitschrift AIT, zunächst als Volontär und Redakteur und dann als Bereichsleiter Corporate Publishing. Neben der Redaktionstätigkeit hält er Vorträge und moderiert Veranstaltungen, vorzugsweise in den Bereichen Nachhaltigkeit und Klimaschutz. Als Großstadtmensch (er lebt seit 2009 in München) ist sein Bezug zum Wohnen in der Landschaft eher theoretischer Natur.

SANDRA HOFMEISTER
is editor-in-chief of DETAIL magazine. After studying history of art and Romance studies in Berlin and Munich, she earned her the Ludwig Maximilians University of Munich. She was editor-in-chief of the German edition of Domus from 2012 to 2015. Her articles on architecture and design have been published in international newspapers, magazines and books. In addition to her work as an editor and publisher, Sandra Hofmeister is a lecturer at the Faculty of Architecture of the Technical University of Munich. She likes to spend her weekends and holidays in the mountains or near the sea. Sandra Hofmeister lives in Munich, Germany.

JAKOB SCHOOF
is editor at Detail, where his responsibilities are chiefly focused on specialised publications and special issues on energy efficiency and sustainability. After studying architecture at the University of Karlsruhe, he worked for the architectural magazine AIT from 2000 to 2009, initially as a trainee, then as editor and finally as divisional director of Corporate Publishing. Apart from editing, he gives lectures and chairs events, preferably in the field of sustainability and climate protection. As a city dweller (he has lived in Munich since 2009), his association with living in the countryside is more of a theoretical nature.

ACME
76 Tabernacle Street
London EC2A 4EA, United Kingdom
acme.ac

Arquitectura-G
Ciutat de Granada 31 2º
08005 Barcelona, Spain
arquitectura-g.com

Aslak Haanshuus Arkitekter
Skedsmogata 14
0655 Oslo, Norway
ahaa.no

Bernardo Bader Architekten
Steinebach 11
6850 Dornbirn, Austria
bernardobader.com

christian pottgiesser architecturespossibles
8, Rue du Pré aux Clercs
75007 Paris, France
pottgiesser.fr

Colorado Building Workshop
1250 14th Street
Denver, CO 80202, USA
coloradobuildingworkshop.com

Cristián Izquierdo architect
Av. Isidora Goyenechea 3356 of. 41
Las Condes, Santiago, Chile
cristianizquierdo.cl

Crosson Architects
L1, 15 Bath Street, PO Box 37-521
Parnell 1052, Auckland, New Zealand
crosson.co.nz

dekleva gregorič arhitekti
Dalmatinova Ulica 11
1000 Ljubljana, Slovenia
dekleva-gregoric.com

Jarmund/Vigsnæs Arkitekter
Henrik Ibsens Gate 100
0255 Oslo, Norway
jva.no

Leth & Gori
Absalonsgade 21B
1658 Copenhagen V, Denmark
lethgori.dk

Morger Partner Architekten AG
Spitalstrasse 8
4056 Basel, Switzerland
morgerpartner.ch

OFIS arhitekti
Tavcarjeva 2
1000 Ljubljana, Slovenia
ofis-a.si

PK Arkitektar
Brautarholt 4
105 Reykjavík, Iceland
pkdm.is

SAMI-arquitectos
Rua Augusto Cardoso, 58 - 2ºandar
2900-255 Setúbal, Portugal
sami-arquitectos.com

studio mk27
Al. Tietê, 505 Jardins - 01417-020
São Paulo, Brasil
studiomk27.com.br

Tegnestuen Vandkunsten
Krudtløbsvej 14
1439 København K, Denmark
vandkunst.dk

Tham & Videgård Arkitekter
Blekingegatan 42,
116 62 Stockholm, Sweden
tvark.se

wespi de meuron romeo architekten
Via G. Branca Masa 9
6578 Caviano, Switzerland
wdmra.ch

Witherford Watson Mann Architects
1 Coate Street,
London E2 9AG, United Kingdom
wwmarchitects.co.uk

Allen, die durch Überlassung ihrer Bildvorlagen, durch Erteilung von Reproduktionserlaubnissen und durch Auskünfte am Zustandekommen des Buches mitgeholfen haben, sagt der Verlag aufrichtigen Dank. Sämtliche Zeichnungen in diesem Werk sind eigens angefertigt oder stammen aus den Archiven der Architekten. Trotz intensiver Bemühungen konnten wir einige Urheber der Abbildungen nicht ermitteln, die Urheberrechte sind aber gewahrt. Wir bitten um dementsprechende Nachricht.

The publisher would like to thank all those who have assisted in the production of this book, be it through providing photos or artwork, or granting permission to reproduce their documents, or providing other information. All the drawings were specially produced for this publication or taken from the archives of the architects. Despite intensive endeavours, we were unable to establish copyright ownership in some cases; however, copyright is assured. Please notify us accordingly in such instances.

Fotografen / Photographers
Aslak Haanshuus Arkitekter: 100/101
Bereuter, Adolf: 46, 48/49, 50
Binet, Hélène: 66, 67
Brygfield, Svein Arne: 128, 1. Einführungsbild
Catrica, Paulo: 20, 102, 104, 105, 106
Devitt, Simon: 52, 54, 55, 56/57
Dupin, George: 42, 44
Gregoric, Ales: 111, 2. Schlußbild
Guerra, Fernando: 120, 122, 123, 124, 125, 2. Einführungsbild
Gustavsen, Tom: 96, 98, 99
Henz, Hannes: 24, 26, 27, 28
Hevia, José: 90, 92, 93, 94/95
Høyer, Helene: 68, 70, 71
Kristinsson, Bjarni: 116/117
Kuroiwa, Jesse: 36, 38,39, 40/41
Larsen, Jan Inge: 126
Lindman, Åke E:son: 58, 60/61, 62, 63
Marolt, Janez: 86, 88, 89
Martincic, Janez: 108, 110, 112/113
Palma, Cristobal: 30, 32, 34/35
Pinho, Rafael: 114, 118, 1. Schlußbild
Rodriguez, Tomás: 72, 74, 76/77
Stamers Kontor / Leth & Gori: 82, 84, 85
Vile, Philip: 64
Walti, Ruedi: 78, 80, 81

Essays:
Villa Noailles
»Visit of the duke of Kent to Charles de Noailles, 1928, Hyères, contemporean print, collection villa Noailles.« 12
Olivier Amsellem 13
Solo Houses project by Christian Bourdais www.solo-houses.com
Bas Princen / Solo Houses 14,15
Pezo Von Ellrichshausen / Solo Houses 16, 17,
Treehotel
Peter Lundström / WDO 18,
Johan Jansson 19
MIT Rotch Visual Collection 131
Wikimedia Commons 140, 141
The Frank Lloyd Wright Foundation Archives (The Museum of Modern Art | Avery Architectural & Fine Arts Library, Columbia University, New York). Acc. no.: 1853.2012.a-d.© 2018. Digital image, The Museum of Modern Art, New York/ Scala, Florence 143
© 2018. VG Bild-Kunst, Bonn

IMPRESSUM

Herausgeberin/Editor
Sandra Hofmeister

Autoren/Authors
Sandra Hofmeister, Jakob Schoof
Sandra Leitte (Projekttexte/Project texts)

Projektleitung/Project management
Eva Herrmann

Lektorat (Deutsch)/Copy editing (German)
Sandra Leitte, Katrin Pollems-Braunfels

Übersetzung/Translation into English
Antoinette Aichele-Platen

Lektorat (Englisch)/Copy editing (English)
Alisa Kotmair

Gestaltung/Design
strobo B M
(Matthias Friederich, Samuel Hinterholzer, Julian von Klier)

Zeichnungen/Drawings
Ralph Donhauser

Reproduktion/Reproduction
Repro Ludwig, AT-5700 Zell am See

Druck und Bindung/Printing and binding
Kessler Druck + Median GmbH + Co. KG

Die für dieses Buch verwendeten FSC-zertifizierten Papiere werden aus Fasern hergestellt, die nachweislich aus umwelt- und sozialverträglicher Herkunft stammen.
The FSC-certified paper used for this book is manufactured from fibres originating from environmentally and socially compatible sources.

FSC www.fsc.org MIX Aus verantwortungsvollen Quellen FSC® C004192

DETAIL – Detail Business Information GmbH, München
www.detail.de

ISBN 978-3-95553-400-4 (Print)
ISBN 978-3-95553-401-1 (E-Book)
ISBN 978-3-95553-402-8 (Bundle)

Bibliografische Information der Deutschen Nationalbibliothek: Die Deutsche Nationalbibliothek verzeichnet diese Publikation in der Deutschen Nationalbibliografie; detaillierte bibliografische Daten sind im Internet über http://dnb.d-nb.de abrufbar.

Bibliographical information published by the German National Library. The German National Library lists this publication in the Deutsche Nationalbibliografie; detailed bibliographical data are available on the Internet at http://dnb.d-nb.de.